Front office operations

FRONT OFFICE OPERATIONS

**(previously
ACCOMMODATION OPERATIONS)**

Third edition

Colin Dix MHCIMA
Chris Baird BA MHCIMA CGLI

Pitman

PITMAN PUBLISHING
128 Long Acre, London WC2E 9AN

© C Dix and C Baird 1988
First published in Great Britain 1988

British Library Cataloguing in Publication Data
Dix, Colin
   Front office operations.—3rd ed.
   1. Receptionists   2. Hotels, taverns, etc.
   —Employees—Great Britain
   I. Title   II. Baird, Chris III. Dix,
   Colin. Accommodation operations
   647'.94   TX930

ISBN0 273 02853 7

Printed and bound in Great Britain

CONTENTS

Contents

PREFACE

The pace of change continues in the hotel industry, and so we have made major alterations to this book to reflect the Industry of the late 80s. Now even the smallest hotel is likely to have an electronic accounting and billing system, and the larger hotels will almost certainly be linked into a worldwide computer system for reservations, and credit card authorisation.

Industrial education keeps pace with the introduction of the new City & Guilds 720 examination for hotel receptionists and this book was prepared with that course in mind. Much of the work is also relevant to the modules of study in BTEC and HCIMA work on hotel reception.

Illustrations are much improved and many of the forms are taken from ones in current use in a variety of UK hotels, so the student can be certain that they are studying the industry as it really is. Still essential is regular reading of trade journals and magazines to keep abreast of the developments in the field of billing, telephone metering systems, and the ownership of the various groups and chains.

The greatest expansion in the book has been in the section concerning sales, as more and more managements recognise the key part the reception department contributes to the profitability of the hotel, where the staff are acknowledged as sales staff rather than clerical staff.

Colin Dix

ACKNOWLEDGEMENTS

I would like to express my thanks to the following organisations for their help, and for their permission to re-produce information, illustrations and documentation.

The Royal Garden Hotel
Dukes Hotel, Bath
Trust House Forte Hotels
Starcrown Hotels
Lloyds Bank, Walthamstow
American Express
Access
Thomas Cook
Canon (UK) Ltd
Tiger Information Systems
Trend Communications Ltd

Thanks are also due to those colleagues who have had made various helpful suggestions, and to Anna Thunhurst for a detailed and constructive review of the first draft.

Chris Killingworth-Baird

Chapter 1

THE HOTEL INDUSTRY AND THE RECEPTION AREA

Chapter objectives

After studying this chapter you should be able to:
- describe how the hotel industry is organised;
- explain the different organisation structures of small, medium and large hotels, and the part the reception department plays in each of them;
- show how the rooms division is organised in a large hotel and the tasks of the employees in each department.

The hotel industry

The Hospitality Industry is made up of various facilities and services for tourists and travellers, and for some countries it represents the most important industry and the biggest single earner of foreign exchange. The hotel sector represents a vital part of these earnings, since the provision of accommodation, food and beverage is essential for anyone spending time away from home, whether it be for business or pleasure.

As the nature of the traveller will vary, so the category of hotel available to them will differ accordingly.

The star rating system is based upon the facilities which the hotel offers, and the service which they provide. This may be as basic as a room with breakfast, or as sophisticated as the service offered in a luxury five-star operation. The facilities offered by a hotel of this nature may include most, or all, of the following:

Room/bathroom en suite
24 hour service in all departments
Radio, TV and video in rooms
Several restaurants
Lounge(s)
Cocktail bar and bar
Room service
Meeting/conference rooms
Banqueting facilities
Valet service

Health club/sauna
Pool
Sports facilities
Cinema
Entertainment
Garaging
Concessions i.e. shops let as kiosks, hairdressers etc.

The decision to stay in a particular hotel may be influenced by various factors. One will certainly be the price. The guest will, however, be influenced by other variables such as the facilities on offer, or the location, or the size.

Many guests have an affinity with a particular group or chain of hotels and always seek out an establishment in which they feel the surroundings are familiar. A chain of hotels generally refers to a number of operations which belong to the same organisation.

INTERNATIONAL CORPORATE HOTELS

These are large chains which are almost household words in the hotel and catering industry (Hilton, Holiday Inns, Inter-Continental). Some of the groups are a combination of company owned, franchise and management contract operations while others are entirely owned by an individual or a company. Their main features include standardisation of service, facilities and price, and many chains endeavour to operate a hotel in most major capitals throughout the world.

MAJOR NATIONAL HOTEL COMPANIES

The UK has its share of international hotels and many of our major national hotel companies are equally well known abroad (Trust House Forte, Crest).

SMALL HOTEL GROUPS

Not all groups of hotels are large or widely dispersed. Some companies own a group which may consist of no more than 4–5 hotels, and they may be confined to a particular area such as the Lake District or the South Coast.

INDEPENDENT HOTELS

These are units which are privately owned or independent of any company. Many guests enjoy staying at an establishment of this nature because of the individuality of the operation. The disadvantage is, of course, that when staying in other towns or countries the guest must find another hotel which suits him and caters for his needs.

HOTEL CONSORTIUM

This system overcomes the disadvantage referred to above since it provides a way for independently owned hotels to affiliate themselves to one another without surrendering their individuality. The advantages to the hotel include shared advertising costs, bulk puchasing and referral of bookings, and to the guest a standardising of quality.

Reception in the hotel organisation

As hotels vary in size, shape and age, so the exact role of the reception department will differ from one hotel to another. The majority of hotels earn the bulk of their revenue and profits from the sale of rooms, so it is essential that the reception department is organised and staffed to maximise sales. Guests, whether staying in a modern 600-room airport hotel or at a small country inn with six rooms, invariably approach the reception desk for information, assistance and answers to any problems they encounter in the hotel.

SMALL HOTELS

In a small hotel the reception will have a number of tasks to carry out. In addition to checking in guests, they will also have to act as secretary and telephonist. A typical organisation structure is shown in Fig. 1.1. In this type of hotel it is probable that all staff members will carry out a variety of jobs; the restaurant waiter will serve in the lounge, and perhaps deliver room service orders, and the manager will probably be responsible for banking, stock-taking, food purchasing and other tasks that would merit separate departments in a larger hotel.

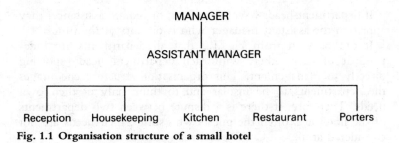

Fig. 1.1 Organisation structure of a small hotel

The assistant manager is unlikely to have a clearly defined responsibility for any area. Normally in the absence of the manager the assistant manager will deputise by covering work usually carried out by the manager. When both are on duty, then the assistant will be allocated tasks on an *ad hoc* basis by the manager.

MEDIUM SIZED HOTELS

As the hotel becomes larger, so it is possible to organise the hotel into more clearly defined departments, each with a department head. Fig. 1.2 shows the organisation structure of a medium sized hotel. The size of the hotel and the length of time that services are open will mean that more staff are required here than in the small hotel. This is also true of management personnel. In a small hotel we have seen that there will be a manager with one assistant. In the medium hotel the post of assistant manager will probably be held by two people. These two assistants will work alternate shifts so that management superivision is provided from 8 a.m. until 11 p.m. seven days a week. One assistant will work 8 a.m. to 4 p.m. and the other 3 p.m. to 11 p.m. The duties of the assistant manager will vary from one hotel to the next but it is rare for the assistant to have any specific duties apart from general supervision.

Fig. 1.2 Organisation structure of a medium sized hotel

If department heads have a problem, or require assistance, they approach the assistant manager who is on duty at the time.

It can be seen from Fig. 1.2 that all departments are independent of each other, with each department head reporting directly to management. This organisation structure encourages the departments to be insular and to think only of their own needs. Therefore, if there is a dispute between two departments of the hotel it is often the guests who suffer; their needs are not considered at all.

LARGE HOTELS

With large hotels of more than 300 rooms it is easier for greater specialisation to occur. This type of hotel can afford to use the skills of full-time accountants, security officers, and personnel managers. Naturally, this means that there is a greater level of professionalism in the different departments and sections of the hotel. Fig. 1.3 shows the management team of a large hotel. The revenue earning sections of the hotel are split into two main divisions. These are 'Food and Beverage', and 'Rooms'.

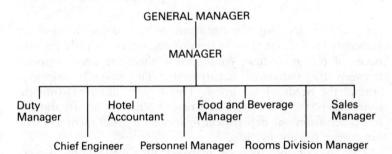

Fig. 1.3 Organisation structure of a large hotel

The managers of these two divisions are members of the management team of the hotel (along with the accountant and other specialists) but obviously they will be responsible for a greater number of people than the other managers.

The management team represents the operating functions of the hotel and is responsible for co-ordinating the various activities that are necessary to the smooth running of a large business. They will work together to organise complex conferences or large package tours that will use the hotel's facilities.

The management team will also carry out the executive functions of the hotel—setting budgets, sales plans, and operating systems will be included in their responsibility. It is common for members of the management team of large hotels of this type to earn more than the manager of a small hotel, for they will be responsible for a larger staff and a far greater turnover.

Fig. 1.4 shows how the rooms division is organised. Co-ordination with other sections of the hotel is achieved by the rooms division manager who is part of the management team. He or she is totally responsible for co-ordination of the individual departments under their control. All of the departments shown in Fig. 1.4 have to work together to make a guest's stay enjoy-

5

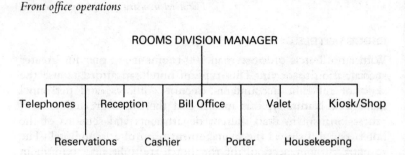

Fig. 1.4 Organisation structure of rooms division in a large hotel

able, and to see that the functions of the rooms division are smoothly carried out. This system of organisation clearly puts the needs of the guest first; consequently there are fewer disputes between the individual departments. The hotel is organised around the needs of the guest. This is very different from the hotel where the guests feel that they are merely an irritation to be pushed from one department to another by staff members who say curtly 'It's not my job.'

The task of the assistant manager in a large hotel is very different from that carried out in a smaller unit. The job title is often 'duty manager', and the main responsibility is dealing with guests. The job is to get problems solved and deal with complaints and queries. But the duty managers are without line authority: they have to resolve the problem through the appropriate member of the management team, or, in their absence, with the department head or supervisor on duty. Duty managers will cover a rota of 24 hours; so for the guest there is always a member of management available to deal with their problems. Often the guest is not aware that they are dealing with a relatively junior member of the management of the hotel, for the duty manager will be an expert at dealing with people and handling complaints.

The general manager in hotels of this size may never see a guest from one week to the next. The job is similar to that of a senior industrial manager; they are responsible for policy, long-term planning and co-ordination of the whole business.

The departments in rooms division

This section will outline the various tasks and responsibilities of the departments that go together to make up the rooms division. Only the largest hotel will have all of these different departments, and in small units many of them will be amalgamated.

HOURS AND SHIFTS

Large hotels really do never close. They have to operate 24 hours a day, 365 days a year. But obviously not every department will operate at full strength all the time. Night duty is from 11 p.m. to 8 a.m. and a separate night staff will be employed to work these hours. Day staff will work either early (8 a.m. to 4 p.m.) or late (3 p.m. to 11 p.m.) and sometimes cover night duty when a permanent member of the night staff is off duty, or on holiday.

Naturally accounts, personnel and other 'office' departments will only operate during normal office hours. Fig. 1.5 shows how a 24 hour coverage of the main departments is provided by key departments, so a restricted service is available even at night for all the rooms division functions. This would also be the case in the food and beverage department.

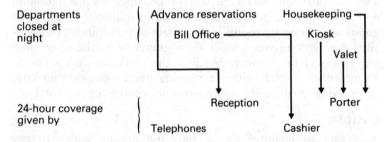

Fig. 1.5 Twenty-four hour coverage of departments in a large hotel

TELEPHONES

The advance of automation is most apparent in the telephone department of large hotels. The number of telephone staff per 100 guests has never been lower. Facilities that can now be carried out without the assistance of an operator include world-wide direct dialling from the guest room, automatic recording of the charge in the bill office, and an automatic early call system. The introduction of the early call system is a particular benefit for it means that every guest can get their call at exactly the right time, something that is not possible with the traditional system where the telephonist may have to make 50 calls at 8 a.m. Obviously, not every one of them could be on the stroke of 8 a.m.

As the switchboard is staffed 24 hours a day, it is also the location of the fire alarms and fire checking equipment. Guest messages may be taken in the telephone room by operators, but often this task is carried out by the porters or reception.

ADVANCE RESERVATIONS

Most bookings will be taken by the advance reservations department; this is normally located near the reception desk, but is not
in view of the guests. This department is usually staffed from
8 a.m. until 6 p.m. as most reservation requests are received
during working hours, with peaks around 10 a.m. and 3 p.m. for
telephone bookings.

Reservation office staff must have a clear speaking voice, but
their appearance and dress do not matter so much, for they do
not come into direct contact with guests. Many hotels use the
advance reservations department as a training ground for people
wishing to work in reception.

RECEPTION

Twenty-four hour coverage will be provided by the reception
desk, but in large hotels the duties are specialised. Checking in
guests and allocating rooms is their main responsibility. Additionally, they will answer queries from guests, and take reservation
requests over the counter. Much of the work involves acting as
an information clerk, either answering guests' question directly,
or referring them to the appropriate department of the hotel.

CASHIER

Accepting payment of guests' bills and dealing with currency
exchange are the major tasks of the cashier. The safe deposit boxes
for guests' valuables will also be located in the office. Other sales
departments of the hotel will receive their floats and pay in their
takings at the cashier's office. The head cashier may prepare the
banking and carry out the paying-in to the bank, but in some
units this will be done by a member of the accounts staff.

Night coverage between 11 p.m. and 8 a.m. is given by a night
auditor who will also post charges, balance the accounting
machines and prepare management reports. The float with which
cashiers may start a shift will probably be in excess of £500, so
it is essential that they are familiar with money and confident in
handling very large sums. Honesty is the prime qualification for
the job and most cashiers will be 'bonded' with an insurance
company so that the hotel is covered against a dishonest act by
one of the cashiers.

BILL OFFICE

This department, like advance reservations, is not a direct guest
contact one. Also, like advance reservations and reception, it is

often used as a proving ground for people who will later work as a cashier. The main task is the posting of charges and payments onto guest bills and extracting summaries of sales figures. Clearly, bill office staff need to be methodical in their working habits and have a grasp of figures, even though much of the work is carried out on computers or accounting machines and calculators.

PORTER

Concierge is the French term for porter, but not every porter comes into this category. Some units separate the department into two, with an enquiry desk and luggage porters. The head porter (*concierge*) is traditionally a person of high status in the hierarchy of the hotel, responsible for guest keys, enquiries, mail, theatre tickets, car hire, baggage and other guest services. Recently, however, many of these tasks have been removed and concessions rented to specialist ticket agencies and car hire companies. Some tourist hotels do not have a head porter at all; instead there is an enquiry desk and luggage handling is supervised from the reception.

VALET

Dry cleaning, pressing and guest laundry are handled by the valet, who reports to the head housekeeper. This job is now only found in the most expensive hotels, as many guests are more willing to wash small items of clothing in the bathroom and borrow an ironing board from the housekeeper.

KIOSK

A shop in the lobby of the hotel will either be operated directly by the hotel, or, more commonly, rented out as a concession to a specialist company. It will sell newspapers, gifts, tobacco and other useful articles. In the concession agreement the hotel will have the right to dictate important points concerning opening hours and the range of goods on sale. They may insist, for example, that the kiosk sells toothbrushes and toilet articles as a service to guests. They may equally refuse permission for some things to be sold, believing that it would not fit the image of the hotel.

HOUSEKEEPING

Numerically, this is the largest department of a hotel, because one maid is needed for every 12–15 rooms. The housekeeper is responsible for the preparation of guest rooms for sale and the cleanliness of all public areas of the hotel. Close liaison between the housekeeper and reception is essential so that rooms are available to let as quickly as possible. Requests for extra blankets or other services are often passed to housekeeping through the reception department. Most housekeeping staff will work between 8 a.m. and 4 p.m., although some maids and a supervisor will be on duty during the evening until 11 p.m. to service the rooms of late departures, carry out cleaning duties, and possibly turn down beds. In some transient hotels 24 hour servicing is provided by the housekeeping department.

Responsibility

All of these departments will have a department head or supervisor who will report to the rooms division manager.

The cashier and bill office staff report to the hotel accountant for matters of operating procedure, training and policy but they are responsible to the rooms manager for their shifts, appearance, and supervision in day to day matters. This split responsibility requires a good working relationship between the rooms manager and the hotel accountant so that there is no conflict in the instructions that are given to the operating staff of the departments.

Career opportunities

The hotel and catering industry has always been renowned for the variety of opportunities which it presents, but recent developments have ensured that today's employees may work in many different settings, doing varied jobs and using a variety of skills.

Most colleges now recognise that a receptionist must have an awareness of the functions of the other areas of the hotel, and many courses now ensure that the front office is seen as part of the whole of the hotel, rather than an isolated section. Most college leavers now have the opportunity to ensure that they are also proficient in many related skills.

Other sectors of the catering and leisure industry where front office staff may seek employment include such outlets as:

- restaurants—traditional or fast food
- wine or cocktail Bars
- public houses
- Clubs—traditional members' clubs or night clubs
- transport catering—flight, ships or trains

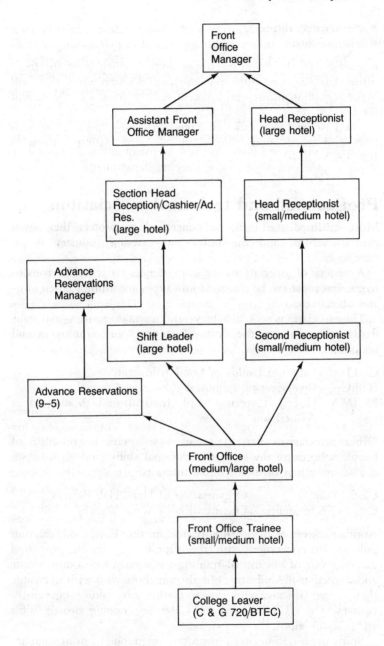

Fig. 1.6 Typical career path

- conference centres
- leisure centres

Regardless of the countless opportunities which exist for front office staff, for most employees the main decision which they will make regarding future employment will be related to the size of the hotel.

The best qualified staff will have had some experience in both large and small hotels, but a typical career path is shown in Fig. 1.6.

Professional and technical associations

Most qualified staff will be concerned to protect their own professionalism, and the hotel and catering industry is no exception.

A variety of associations are in existence, far too numerous to name, but most can be classified into types according to their aims and objectives.

The associations seek to achieve and maintain professional standards by examining the skills of students and employees and include:

CGLI   City and Guilds of London Institute
BTEC   Business and Technical Education Council
HCIMA   Hotel, Catering and Institutional Management Association

Other associations may represent a voluntary organisation of people who share the same occupational skills, and wish to see the advancement of their mutual interests:

Clefs D'Or   Organisation of Head Hall Porters
Guild of Sommeliers Organisation of Wine Waiters

Another association of importance in the hotel and catering industry is concerned with the supervising, encouraging and carrying out of vocational training—not only for young people about to enter the industry, but also for those who wish to change their career, or those who wish to further it by taking supervisory courses. The HCTB (Hotel and Catering Training Board) fulfils all these functions.

Some organisations exist to protect the public from malpractice and to encourage their members to observe a professional code and behaviour, i.e.

ABTA   Association of British Travel Agents
BHRA   British Hotel and Restaurants Association

Organisations such as trade unions have a steadily increasing membership among the workforce, and seek to improve the working conditions and payment for hotel and catering employees. The principal unions are:

GMWU   General & Munical Workers Unions
TGWU   Transport and General Workers Union

Many associations will perform more than one function, for example the HCIMA does not only seek to examine students and maintain standards, but also provides a wide variety of services for members, both professional and social, and through a magazine enables many employees to keep up to date with developments all over the world. Most Hotel and Catering employees will be a member of at least one association or organisation during their career, and some will join several, either to protect their interests or to further their social and professional contacts

Self assessment questions

1 List the facilities which you would expect to find in a five-star hotel.
2 Differentiate between the different categories of hotels
3 Explain the difference in management structure between a medium and a large hotel.
4 What are the main tasks of a receptionist in a small hotel?
5 List other important sections of the hotel and catering industry where Front Office Staff may gain employment.
6 Name three technical or professional associations and explain their function.

Chapter 2

THE RECEPTIONIST
AND THE LAW

Chapter objectives

After studying this chapter you should be able to:
- identify the necessary personal qualities of an efficient hotel receptionist;
- explain how good personal presentation can enhance the work of a hotel receptionist;
- outline the main points of how a hotel receptionist would need to carry out his or her duties.

The receptionist

An amusing mnemonic suggests that all receptionists should be DRIPS—although not in the literal sense! It categorises the role of the receptionist into five areas.

1 Diplomat.
2 Record keeper.
3 Information source.
4 Psychologist.
5 Salesperson.

What skills are required for carrying out the work of a receptionist and how can they be recognised?

Most hotel staff are recruited after an interview. The picture that an interview gives, however, is often only a partial view of the applicant, for the person applying for the job may try and minimise the traits that they feel would debar them from work as a receptionist.

A list of attributes for the 'perfect' receptionist often sounds similar to those required for perfection in any person (or any other customer-contact job). There is much discussion over whether or not it is possible to train employees to be smart, socially skilled, diplomatic, systematic and so on.

Possibly the most important requirement for the receptionist is the ability (and willingness) to learn. It is unlikely that a recluse will apply to work where they would be in constant contact with people, so, in this respect, applicants will be self-selecting.

A foreign language may be a useful asset in international hotels, but for the bulk of the hotels in the UK a good, clear command of the English language would be adequate. Foreign language needs may be met in smaller hotels by other members of staff, or the provision of phrase books, which invariably deal with the needs of hotel guests.

SOCIAL SKILLS

Social skills have been described as the way in which a person behaves towards others in different social situations. This can be characterised by the difference between a receptionist's behaviour towards a VIP guest and his or her behaviour towards the page who has been detailed to accompany the guest to the room. The receptionist will adopt a different style in each case.

Social skills are achieved by the co-ordination of verbal and non-verbal behaviour in a given situation. Equally important is the perception of cues from the other person.

To gain an assessment of a person, it is normal to evaluate information not only from what is said, but the way in which it is said, the bearing or posture, and the gestures the person makes. In addition, important clues are gained from clothing, accessories and luggage. All of this is co-ordinated, often subconsciously, to produce an assessment. For the receptionist, this is very important. Within a few moments, a receptionist may have to decide whether or not to request a deposit. In sales, too, the ability to sum up a customer quickly is important. Should the guest be offered a more expensive room? Or should 'value for money' be emphasised?

Airline companies train their staff to quickly recognise passengers who are showing signs of nervousness, and to handle them with extra care to give them reassurance.

Social skills like any other skill can be acquired. They deal with feelings and behaviour: it is essential that careful attention is given to any training programme that includes training in social skills. For a receptionist, certain simple social skills are easily acquired. The first is an **attentive manner**. In listening to a customer, the receptionist should be interested and concerned about what is being said; it is also important not to fiddle with a pencil or to move things around on the desk—these actions quickly show boredom. The second is **eye contact**. It is remarkable that some front office staff manage to deal with guests without ever looking them in the eye. The impression again is one of disinterest and shallowness. Eye contact should be established and used throughout any dealings with guests. The third is **tone of voice**. This can convey meanings as effectively as what is said; it is not enough to say, 'I am sorry, sir,'—it must be said with the correct inflexion of speech. For most people, a pleasant voice is not too loud and not too fast. An alarming trait is that of shouting at foreigners in the hope that they will understand through the sheer volume of noise. The fourth is the **use of guests' names**. At every opportunity the guest's name should be used. This personalises the conversation, and is clear evidence of interest and personal attention. In addition, it assists reception staff in remembering the names of individual guests. Some hotel companies train their front office staff to address the guest by name at least three times during registration. Conversely, it is extremely rude to refer to guests by their room number, such as, '309 would like to know how much his bill is'. Even in large hotels, it is possible to use guests' names by glancing quickly at the room status system or the key card when being asked for a room key.

HANDLING COMPLAINTS

A specialised and important applied social skill is that of dealing with complaints from guests. Normal responses often follow the pattern of 'It's not my fault', 'Oh no I didn't', 'It wasn't me' and other similar phrases. All that these achieve is the provocation of further argument. In dealing with complaints the receptionist should follow these points:

1 listen attentively: it is necessary to show that attention is being given;
2 do not interrupt: an interruption will encourage the complainant to carry on louder and longer;
3 wait until the person has completely finished: before saying anything at all, be certain that the guest has completely finished talking, rather than just taking a pause for breath;
4 apologise: a short clear apology should be the first thing the receptionist offers. It should be clear and concise, and not qualified in any way by an excuse or explanation;
5 speak normally: a guest complaining is often further aggravated by a receptionist whose voice rises to match that of the irate guest. The result is an unseemly slanging match which can be watched by other guests and staff members;

6 summarise the complaint: repeating the essence of a complaint serves two purposes; firstly, it ensures that everything has been covered and that there has been no misunderstading about the cause of the complaint; secondly, a factual dispassionate summary helps to defuse the situation as it cannot produce further dispute; 7 explain what action will be taken and how quickly: it is important when giving an explanation of action that the guest is not given the impression that 'buck passing' is being carried out. By giving a definite time, the guest is encouraged that something will be done about the grievance.

If a guest is particularly irate, the receptionist should aim to remove the scene to somewhere more private, such as an office, or adjacent lounge. In doing this, the receptionist will also remove the physical barrier of the reception desk from the confrontation, for a desk or table can also be a psychological barrier.

PERSONAL PRESENTATION

All the above attributes help to contribute to the overall impression of the receptionist and the hotel. Good social skills will not only increase self confidence and effectiveness, but will also create a favourable impression of the hotel, and inspire customer confidence in the receptionist and the department. A neat and tidy appearance is obviously important in order to convey that vital good first impression. A receptionist should aim to be clean, neatly clothed and well groomed. Many hotels now provide staff with a uniform. For male staff this is often a business suit, with a pastel shirt and company tie, although many hotels have once again reverted to the traditional pin stripe suits, with white shirt and grey tie. In a very few luxury hotels it is still customary for the male reception and management staff to change into dinner jackets during the evening shift.

Uniform for female staff is more varied, and may be a neat tailored dress, a blouse and skirt or a smart suit. Sometimes different grades of staff are given variations of a basic uniform style, which serves to show their status in the organisation. Whatever the uniform a receptionist should ensure that it is kept as clean and well pressed as if it were their own clothing. If the selection of the clothing is left to the receptionist it is important that it is smart and business–like, yet comfortable. The latest fashions frequently look out of place in the work situation and it is wise to choose something which is traditional and in keeping with the environment. Particular attention should be paid to accessories and jewellery. As a general rule they should be kept to a minimum, especially if a uniform is worn, since they can easily detract from the overall effect of unformity which should characterise front office staff.

Receptionists and the law

This section will cover the main points of law with which a receptionist should be directly involved. With the exception of the manager, a receptionist is the member of staff who is most likely to need knowledge of the law relating to the operation of a hotel and the handling of guests.

HOTELS IN LAW

The first problem is, what is a hotel? The Hotel Proprietors Act 1956 lays down responsibilities for 'inns'. Most hotels offering accommodation, even the most luxurious establishment in Park Lane, will be classed as inns. Even though an establishment is called an inn, it may not fall within the realm of the Act, for there may be no accommodation to let. Private hotels are the other category. Once again, the name cannot be taken as a guide; some establishments entitled 'Private Hotel' may in reality be inns. Generally, private hotels are those establishments that choose their guests in some way or other, perhaps by offering accommodation to clergymen only. Finally, the display of the sign limiting liability for loss to guests' property does not indicate that the property is an inn because the notice itself contains a disclaimer (*see below*).

BOOKING

Bookings and reservations are covered by the law of contract.

The first stage is the offer. A potential guest enquires whether or not accommodation is available on a given night. The receptionist states that there is room available at £30, for example; the offer has been made.

Next is the acceptance; the guest can either accept the offer, reject it, or make a counter offer. If they accept, then the contract is formed. There is no need for written confirmation in law. Naturally, a verbal contract will be more difficult to prove, but it is a contract, none the less.

Cancellation of bookings is in favour of the guest: if they wish to cancel a booking, the cancellation takes effect the moment they post the letter of cancellation. Should the hotel wish to withdraw, its letter of cancellation does not take effect until it is received by the guest.

Certain groups of people have only limited rights to make contracts. The ones most relevant to hotels are: persons under the age of eighteen, the mentally sick, drunkards, and companies.

REGISTRATION

Guests at a hotel must provide their full name and nationality. They are not obliged to provide the information themselves; for example, it could be given by a tour leader or chauffeur, nor are they legally obliged to sign a register. Aliens have to provide, in addition, details of their passport number and its place of issue, their next destination and the address there if known.

All of this information has to be kept for twelve months. In law there is no requirement for a guest to provide an address, nor even their real name. Naturally, a hotel would be very cautious of a guest who was unwilling to provide their address, or of a guest who they thought may be using a false name, although this may be common practice amongst celebrities.

Every guest must register, so it is insufficient for Mr and Mrs John Smith to check into a hotel. The full name of Mrs Smith has to be provided. The record of guests must be produced to a police officer on request, but if required for any other purpose, need only be provided after a court order.

All this is outlined in the Immigration (Hotel Records) Order 1972 and applies both to inns and to private hotels. The exceptions to this are diplomats, their families and staff who are exempted by the Diplomatic Privileges Act 1964.

Hotels have to accept every traveller that arrives, unless there is a special case for refusal. This may be if the person is in an unfit state to be received, or if the hotel is full. The category 'unfit to be received' would include guests who were drunk. Colour or nationality are not sufficient reasons to refuse to receive guests; this area is covered in the Race Relations Act 1976. A guest who arrived with a known prostitute could also be refused, for it would open the hotel to prosecution as an immoral house.

To avoid argument over such points as when a person is drunk, or who is a prostitute, the safest course for receptionists to follow is to refuse a guest because the hotel is full. There can then be no question of doubt about the guest's fitness to be received.

The hotel is entitled in common law to request that the guest pays a reasonable amount in advance; there is no obligation to allow guests credit. Many hotels request a deposit greater than one night's room charge to cover the use of extras such as telephones, or the restaurant.

PRICE DISPLAY

The Tourism (Sleeping Accommodation Price Display) Order 1977, which came into operation in 1978, requires all hotels and guest houses to display their tariff at the reception desk. This order ensures that the rate for each type of room is clearly shown and that the amount of any taxes and service charges are also displayed. If meals are included this also has to be made clear.

Service charges must not be stated as a percentage of the rate, but included in the price charged; so a typical notice may say:

Single room—£40 per night including VAT and service charge.
Double room—£56 per night including VAT and service charge.
Suites—£80–£180 per night including VAT and service charge.

INNKEEPERS' LIABILITY

The hotel is liable for loss of guests' property while they are staying at the hotel (strictly, from midnight on the day of arrival to midnight on the day of departure), but is not liable for guests' cars or their contents.

This liability does not extend to cases where loss or damage is

---

NOTICE

LOSS OR DAMAGE TO GUESTS' PROPERTY

Under the Hotel Proprietors Act 1956, a hotel proprietor may in certain circumstances be liable to make good any loss or damage to a guest's property even though it was not due to any fault of the proprietor or staff of the hotel.

The liability however
(a) extends only to the property of guests who have engaged sleeping accommodation at the hotel;

(b) is limited to £50 for any one article and a total of £100 in the case of any one guest, except in the case of property which has been deposited, or offered for deposit, for safe custody;

(c) does not cover motor cars or other vehicles of any kind or any property left in them, or horses, or other live animals.

This notice does not constitute an admission either that the act applies to this hotel or that liability thereunder attaches to the proprietor of this hotel in any particular case.

Fig. 2.1 Schedule of Hotel Proprietors Act 1956

caused by an act of God, action by the Queen's enemies, or negligence by the guest or their servants or companions.

If the loss is caused by negligence or action of the hotelier or the staff then the hotel is fully liable, even if it has limited its liability through displaying the statutory notices from the Hotel Proprietors Act 1956. This notice limits the liability of the hotel to £50 for any one article, or a total of £100 per guest. It is printed in full in Fig. 2.1.

Section (b) is important for it shows that liability can be full if the property was put into safe deposit or offered for safe deposit.

If a guest were to offer property for deposit, but the receptionist refused it as all deposit boxes were full, and it was subsequently stolen, then the hotel would be fully liable for the subsequent loss.

The goods lost do not have to belong to guests for them to be able to claim. A salesperson could claim for lost samples, for example.

PAYMENT OF BILL

A hotel may request full payment of the bill in legal tender. In practice this means cash. An offer to pay by any other means need only be accepted at the discretion of the hotel. The Theft Act 1968 has made it easier for guests who leave without paying to be prosecuted. Section 16 allows prosecution of any person who obtains a pecuniary advantage by deception. A guest who gives a cheque in payment, knowing that it will not be met, can be prosecuted. If it is given in good faith, however, this may not be the case.

INNKEEPER'S LIEN

Should a guest be unable or unwilling to pay the bill, the hotel may hold the guest's property against payment. Excluded from this are cars and the clothing worn by the guest. This does not mean that a guest may be physically restrained from leaving the hotel, for the restraint may constitute an assault.

All the guest's property may be held, even if it is clear that it will more than cover the amount of the bill. There is no need to bargain over the amount that should be left.

The Innkeepers Act 1878 allows the hotelier to auction the goods after six weeks. The auction must be advertised at least one month previously. Any surplus that remains from the sale after deducting the amount of the bill and expenses should be returned to the guest.

Value added tax

VAT is a government tax which is levied on most goods and services, with the exclusion of things such as newspapers and VPOs. Any service charge which is added to the total bill will also be subjected to VAT.

Accurate records must be maintained of all VAT collected and since prices are frequently shown inclusive of VAT the reception staff must learn to become adept at extracting VAT from the price quoted. Officers from HM Customs and Excise are free to inspect the hotel VAT records at any time.

Self assessment questions

1 What are the main attributes of a hotel receptionist?
2 Give the main points to follow when handling a guest complaint.
3 Why is good personal presentation important?
4 Outline the main points of law concerning the registration of guests.
5 How much can a hotel limit its liability for the loss of guests' property?

Chapter 3

RESERVATIONS

Chapter objectives

After studying this chapter you should be able to:
- identify the sources of reservations;
- show how they are recorded and charted prior to the guests arrival at the hotel.

Methods of reservation

All hotels accept reservations or advance bookings for their rooms, in order to achieve high occupancy, and maximise their revenue. The proportion of advance reservations will vary from 100% in a resort hotel to perhaps 10% in a 'transient' or motorway hotel. Also, the length of time in advance that the guest books (the 'lead' time) will vary from a few hours to many months.

The reception staff need a system which will enable them to:

1 check if a reservation request is possible;
2 record the booking;
3 retrieve the booking at the appropriate time.

It does not matter how the request for a reservation is made; the system of processing it will remain the same. All possible forms a reservation request can take are shown in Fig. 3.1.

The immediate request is 'a room for tonight', but the future request could be for 'next week', 'next month' or even 'next year'.

TELEPHONE

Telephone bookings are the most common in many hotels. It is quick, most people have access to a phone, and most importantly, it is interactive—the potential guest can find out immediately if a room is available, if the price is satisfactory, and so on. It also gives the receptionist the opportunity to clarify any necessary points—who will be paying the bill, will the arrival be before 6 p.m., is there a restaurant booking wanted and so on.

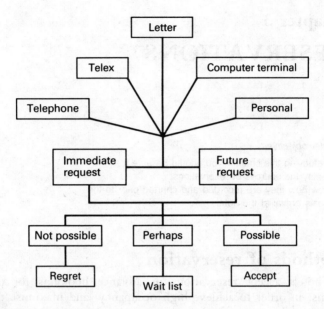

Fig. 3.1 Reservation alterations

Normally, telephone reservations are requested to confirm the booking.

TELEX

The telex combines the speed of the telephone with the permanence of a letter. Most larger hotels now have a telex in the reservations department. There is less opportunity for misunderstanding a reservation request, a confirmation of booking is instantaneous, and it is still interactive—the reservation clerk can converse with the customer. Another important advantage of the telex in reservations departments is that a message can still be sent even though there is no-one on duty at the other end. This is particularly important for hotels with an international clientele. A guest may book from Australia or America without having to check time zones to ensure that someone will be available to take the reservation. Equally, the hotel can telex back a confirmation at any time it wishes.

LETTER

Resort hotels have much of their accommodation reserved by letter. The lead time is longer, so speed of communication is not so important. A letter of reservation is also useful, for the customer can tell the hotelier on arrival about any special requests, and it is clearly more enforceable as a contract in the event of a subsequent non-arrival.

If the guests wish to charge the account to their company then this can be mentioned in the letter, and the hotel has authorisation which it can verify if necessary.

COMPUTER TERMINAL

The majority of hotel groups now operate their reservations department by the extensive use of computers, for example THF has its own computer network ensuring fast and informative data regarding reservations throughout the entire group. Many systems additionally enable contact to be made very quickly with other organisations should the need occur. Normally the computer information is updated by each unit, and the program is set so that if one hotel or room type is full it will automatically offer the closest alternative. With these systems the updating of reservations is instantaneous. The linking of hotel reservation systems with airline networks and the connection through Prestel to travel agents and hotel booking agents have ensured that advance bookings made by computer terminal have become simpler and faster than ever before.

PERSONAL

Here there is a direct face to face contact between the customer and the receptionist. Return bookings are frequently made in this way as guests depart at the end of their stay. The receptionist has the opportunity to find out the maximum information (about late arrival or room type required) and can answer any queries the guest may raise. At quiet times the receptionist may also be able to show the guest the room type and utilise some sales techniques to increase the expenditure of the potential customer.

OVERSEAS TELEGRAMS AND CABLES

The use of this service has certainly declined with the growth of computer networks and increased use of telex, but it is still util-ised by some companies and individuals to make last minute bookings or amendments.

Recording the reservation

All the systems used to record bookings should be kept out of the view of guests. This avoids the desk looking cluttered and untidy and also helps security.

If the hotel is able to accept a booking, then it has to be recorded. This is normally done by noting the requirements on a reservation form and entering the details in the diary. All details of bookings for a particular day are then kept together.

RESERVATION FORM

Telephone and personal bookings are normally noted on a standard reservation form. The use of a form for this purpose has many benefits:

1 it acts as a check list to ensure that all the relevant information is obtained;
2 it is a reminder to tell the guest certain things, (price, release time etc.);
3 it can be easily processed;
4 it is less likely to be lost.

The layout of the form in a logical manner is important, and the use of boxes will speed completion (*see* Fig. 3.2).

ROOM RESERVATION

NAME SPARROW G. Mr — ARRIVAL 23/6
NAME — DEPARTURE 24/6
NAME — Refile Arrival
Departure

SINGLE ☑ RATE £40 — ARRIVAL TIME 23.00
TWIN ☐ RATE
DOUBLE ☐ RATE — GUARANTEED (YES) NO
EXEC. ☐ RATE
SUITE: ☐ — PAST GUEST ☑
TYPE RATE
TYPE RATE — Mkt Seg.

RESERVATION REQUESTED BY Jan — PHONE 01 246 2648 x 123
COMPANY Birds Ltd — TOWN London
ADDRESS 10 Wellend Walk

REMARKS GTD Late Arr. 2140 - Heathrow

BILL TO Birds Ltd — ACCOUNT NO: ☐☐☐☐☐

PHONE ☑ VERBALLY ☐ DATE 1/6 — RESERVATION TAKEN BY CKB
TO BE CONFIRMED BY TELEX ☑ BY LETTER ☐ NOT ☐ — COMPUTER REF:

Fig. 3.2 Room reservation

Some hotels combine the reservation form with the Registration Card on the other side so that all the relevant information is available together (*see* Fig. 3.3).

Length of stay	CASH ☐			**EROS HOTEL**
	CHEQUE ☐			69 SHAFTESBURY AVENUE LONDON W1V 8EX
Number in party	A/C ☐			Telephone: 01-734 8781 Telex: 268564 EROSHT
	CREDIT CARD ☐			
	VOUCHER ☐			

MR.
MRS.
MISS _____ Please Print in Full

Address _____

_____

_____ City _____

Country _____ Nationality _____ Car Registration Number _____

Passport No.
(Aliens only) _____ Where Issued _____

Next Destination
(Give address) _____

ACCOUNT CUSTOMERS ONLY — If the Company for whatever reason fails to honour this account, I undertake to be held personally liable for the full payment thereof.

Receptionist | Signature

	a.m.			
Arr:	p.m.	Name		Room No.
Dep		Rate	Acc Requested	Length of stay

				Deposit
Letter				
Telex				Receipt No.
Cable	Date booking made	Receptionist		
Counter	Booked by			Voucher No.
Telephone				
Chance	A/c to.			
Regular				
T.B.C.				
N.T.B.C.				

Remarks

Fig. 3.3 Reservation/registration form

HOTEL DIARY

All reservations are entered in the hotel diary under the arrival date. The diary is normally a large, loose-leaf ledger which is constantly updated by the addition of new pages at the back, and the pages for each day's arrivals are removed from the front. A

NAME	TYPE OF ROOM	NO. OF NIGHTS	RATE	DATE	CONFIRM-ATION	ROOM NO.	REMARKS
Finch Mr. C ⎫ Hawks Mr. M ⎭	TB	3	£45	19/2	Tlx		Quiet.
Jay Mrs. P.	Suite	4	£80	11/3	C/F		V.I.P.
Sparrow Mr. G.	SB	1	£30	19/4	C/F.		A/c to Birds
Robin Miss R.	SB	2	£30	16/5			See also 24/5+ '9/7
~~Starling Mr. H~~	TB	3	£45	16/5			~~Canc. T 18/5~~
Nightingale Tours.	15TB 3DB	4	–	20/3			ARR. 18.00. Buffet 19.30.

WED.   10th June

Fig. 3.4 Extract from diary

fresh page is used for each day and if it becomes full, a follow-on page can be easily inserted. The reservation form in Fig. 3.2 has a box for the clerk to tick when the booking has been transferred to the diary. Letter and telex reservations are normally entered straight into the diary.

It can be seen from Fig. 3.4 that reservations are entered chronologically, so to look for a particular name on a given day's arrival sheet may take some moments. The remarks column allows the reservation clerk to note any special requirements, such as the account to company of 'Mr Sparrow', and also any subsequent cancellations, and the date of cancellation. This is shown for 'Mr Starling'. Tour or group bookings are normally entered in the diary in the same way as a normal booking, although they obviously represent a larger number of arrivals. If a booking is for two or more people with different names, both names are always noted, so that if mail or messages arrive for the guest the receptionist is aware of the arrival date.

Multiple dates
'Miss Robin' has reserved accommodation on two other dates in addition to 23rd June. All of these are noted in the diary under each arrival date with cross references to all the others. In this way the receptionist has the maximum information available. The letter booking the accommodation can either be moved forward to the next date after each arrival, or if possible, photocopies and a copy should be placed under each arrival date.

Rack system

A rack system can operate both room status and also advance reservations, each of which can be installed independently of each other—a hotel operating a reservation rack does not necessarily have to compliment it with the room status system.

A Whitney system is an example of a rack system.

Advance reservations filed in a rack system operate in basically the same way as the reservation diary, but instead of bookings being entered into the diary they are entered on a 'rack slip' (sometimes called a 'shannon') and this rack slip is filed visibly under the date of arrival. The big advantage over the diary is that reservations can be filed alphabetically. Checks can be made very quickly to see if a guest has a reservation (*see* Fig. 3.5).

The reservation slip is filled out for every booking and put into a metal carrier. This is stored in the 'reservation rack' under the

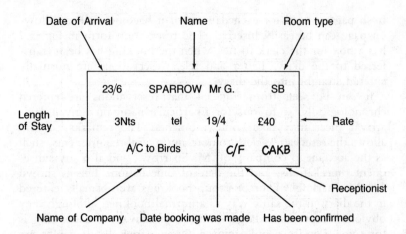

Date of Arrival   Name   Room type

23/6   SPARROW Mr G.   SB

Length of Stay → 3Nts   tel   19/4   £40 ← Rate

A/C to Birds   C/F CAKB

→ Receptionist

Name of Company   Date booking was made   Has been confirmed

Fig. 3.5 Rack reservations slip

arrival date. Strict alphabetical order can be maintained right up to the day of arrival.

Figure 3.6 shows a section of the reservation rack for the 23 June. If this is compared with the diary section (*see* Fig. 3.4) it is easy to see the benefit of the alphabetical filing of the reservations. Tour entries are also entered into individual rack slips in the same way as other bookings. As with the reservation diary, if a booking is cancelled, it is not removed, but simply crossed through. This is shown for the booking of 'Mr Starling'. These reservation racks are stored on the walls of the reservation office in full view of all reservation clerks. They will extend as long as the period of time over which bookings extend. In a 500-room hotel, the rack for the next·day's arrivals may have over 100 separate rack slips filed in it. But the rack for a year ahead may have only one rack slip for the whole month of June. The display of the racks does mean that reservation staff have a much clearer picture of the future bookings than when the information is stored in the traditional diary.

When the slips are filed in the rack only the top line with the most important information shows.

Colour coding
Some hotels colour code reservation slips so that easy visual checks may be made of a day's reservation profile. Systems will vary, but a suitable one could be:

23rd June		
Arr. Date 23/6	Name Finch, Mr. C.	Room TB
Arr. Date 23/6	Name Hawks, Mr. H.	Room With Finch
Arr. Date 23/6	Name Jay, Mr. P.	Room Suite
Arr. Date 23/6	Name Nightingale Gp.	Room 15T 3D
Arr. Date 23/6	Name Robin, Miss R.	Room SB
Arr. Date 23/6	Name Sparrow, Mr. G.	Room SB
Arr. Date 23/6	Name Starling	Room TB
Dep. Date 26/6	Account 18/5	Rate £25
Conf. Date 16/5 Cancelled.		
Letter ☑	Telex ☐	Telephone ☐

Fig. 3.6 Part of reservation rack

1 pink = VIP;
2 blue = tour;
3 white = ordinary;
4 yellow = travel agent.

This diary-keeping is perfect for computerisation, and many companies offer it for use on small microcomputers.

RESERVATIONS

A diary is the most basic form of reservation system. It records the bookings as they come in. The next stage up is Whitney where the reservations can be continually kept in alphabetical order and removed if cancelled or amended. A computer system simply reproduces the function of the diary. The procedure is shown below.

Reservation procedure

Traditional method		Task	Equipment
Check chart		Check chart	VDU
Enter on reservation form		┌Enter booking	Keyboard
Enter in diary	Simultaneous	├Update chart	Memory
Update chart		├Send confirmation	Word processor
Send confirmation		└Store	Memory
File			

Traditional method   *Computer method*

If the booking is cancelled then a simple command to the computer will reverse the process. Depending upon how the program is written the screen may still display the booking but distinguish it as cancelled. This facility to continue to display a booking may be very useful for amended arrival dates. As all the processes are completed simultaneously the accuracy and speed of charts, reservation letters, and amendments are improved dramatically.

Overbooking too can become more scientific, as the computer may be programmed to record the relationship between reservations and actual arrivals, and even the likelihood of different classes of booking not arriving.

Finally an up-to-the-minute arrival list can be prepared and printed for distribution, although if the hotel has a number of VDUs in use then these can display the arrival list as required.

CHARTING RESERVATIONS

It is necessary to make sure that there is a room available to sell, however a reservation is recorded. The position for any date in the future needs to be completely accurate. If it is overstated the request will be refused when space is available, and if all bookings are not recorded, then inadvertent overbooking may occur.

The booking chart has to be checked to establish whether or not it is possible to accept a reservation, or if it has to be put on the waiting list or even refused.

The procedure for taking a booking is shown in Fig. 3.7. Once again, no matter how the request for a booking is received, the reservation clerk will have to follow through each step of the procedure.

All reservation charts follow the principle of showing the number of 'room nights' there are available in the hotel. This is done for each specific room on a 'conventional chart' or for groups of rooms on a 'density chart'.

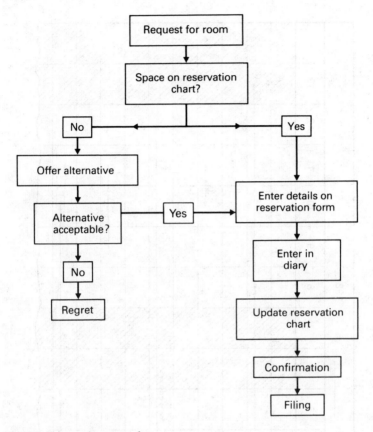

Fig. 3.7 Reservation procedure

CONVENTIONAL CHART

The conventional chart shows each room in the hotel individually. The room type is noted next to the room number. The chart is usually used in smaller hotels, where room types may differ substantially. It is particularly common in the older resort hotel which has the following characteristics:

1 a great variety of room types;
2 a long average guest stay (three or more nights);
3 a long lead time of reservations;
4 some repeat business.

The chart functions by the receptionist allocating a room at the time of booking and noting this in the diary. An entry is made

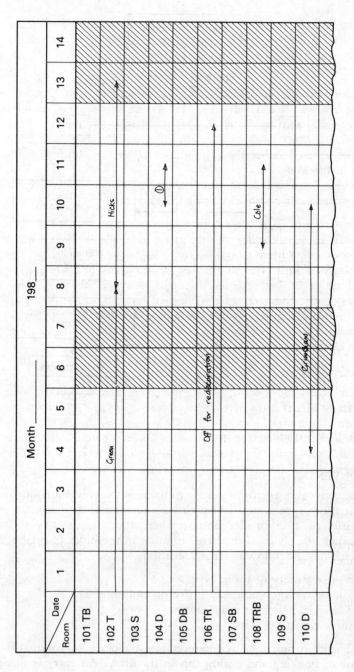

Fig. 3.8 Conventional reservation chart

on the chart in pencil, with the name of the guest or a reference number by the booking. Weekends and Bank Holidays can be shown by shading (*see* Fig. 3.8).

Certain guidelines must be followed. These are:

1 entries must be made in pencil so that alteration can be made;
2 the arrows should run from the centre of each day as this corresponds with the hotel 'day' of midday to midday;
3 if it is a short booking then the folio number from the diary should be used rather than the guest's name (*see* Room 104 on 10th in Fig. 3.8);
4 chance bookings, extensions of stay, rooms off and early departures must be noted so that the chart is always accurate.

This form of chart is ideal for the smaller hotel, but it becomes difficult to see whether or not space is available as the hotel becomes full. Often a booking may be taken by 'juggling' the existing bookings. This means that an entry may be changed two or three times before guests actually arrive at the hotel and consequently, they are not informed of their room number until they actually register. A conventional chart can be very time-consuming to keep up-to-date, and lower occupancy often results from errors.

DENSITY CHART

Larger hotels use a density chart to record their bookings. With the density chart rooms are classified into groups of a similar type and no allocation of a specific room is made until the guest arrives at the hotel. This is ideal for modern hotels where all rooms are similar, with only the floor level and view from the window changing. The density chart is also more useful where the guest stay is short, for entries can be quickly made and changed if necessary. As with the conventional chart, chance bookings, extensions, early departures, all have to be noted on the chart to make sure it is a true picture of the reservation position. This is often checked by the reservations manager, who can compare the number of rooms let on the chart, with the actual number of guests in the hotel (and due to arrive) on a given day.

DENSITY RESERVATION CHART

Figure 3.9 shows a density reservation chart in which each page represents one week and the pages are headed with the month and dates and stored in a loose leaf binder. Entries are made in pencil. Tours are entered quickly by ruling off the appropriate number

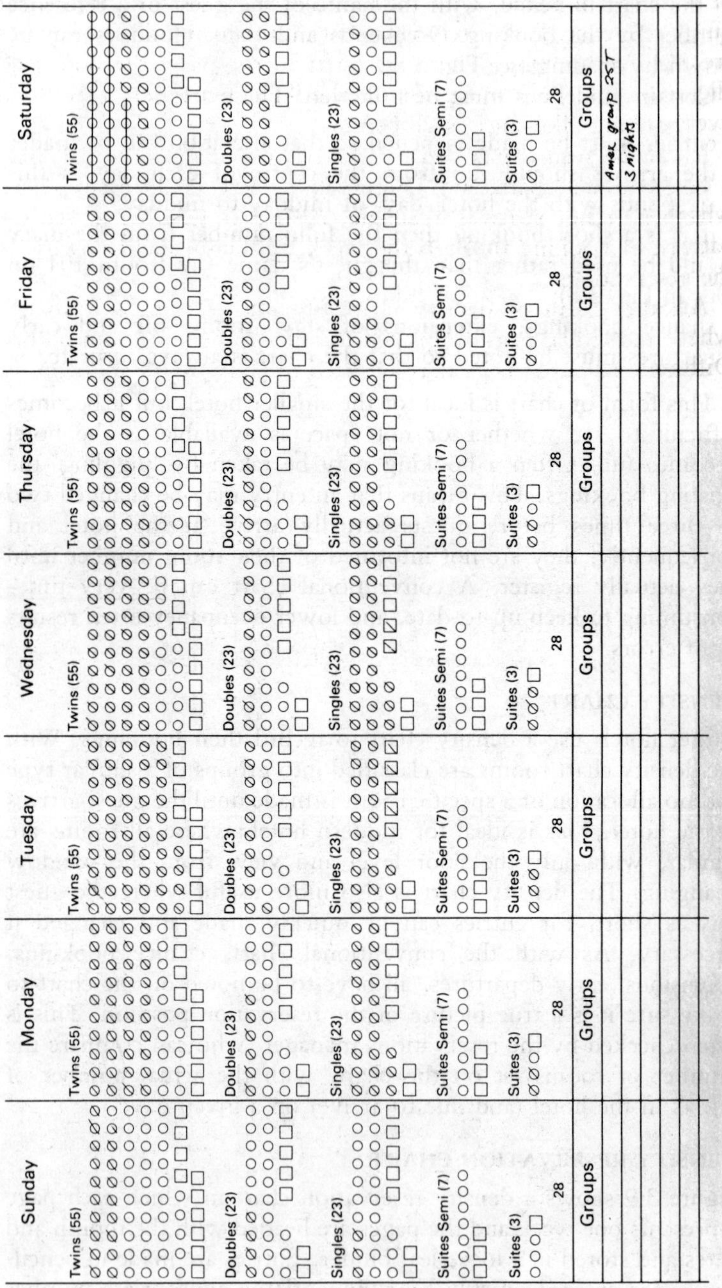

Fig. 3.9 Density reservation chart

of rooms. The name of the tour is entered on the bottom line for quick reference. Each circle represents a 'room night'. The squares are for overbooking. There are 55 twin rooms in the hotel and allowance has been made for overbooking ten twins. (The total overbooking allowance is 28 rooms.)

It can be seen that a density chart is much more 'visual' than a conventional chart, and a reservation clerk could easily check whether or not space is available. Also it is possible to see the pattern of booking through the week by the 'ups and downs' of the reservations.

Another form of density chart often used is a 'peg board', where individual pegs are placed in holes to denote room nights. Different coloured pegs may be used to show tours and groups.

Fig. 3.10

This form of chart is easy to update. For a cancellation, the appropriate pegs are removed.

Again many hotel computer systems offer charting as part of a reservation package. It is important that the flow of bookings is catered for in the display method. The display should ideally echo a traditional density chart.

STOP-GO CHART

In large hotels there would be a bottleneck if every reservation clerk had to refer to the booking chart every time they handled a reservation request. This is overcome by a visual 'stop-go' chart which is prominently displayed in the reservation office. This chart summarises the information on the main chart. It shows at a glance whether or not to accept a booking. There is space for each day of the year.

Figure 3.11 shows a section of a stop-go chart. From this it can be seen that there are no single rooms available on 6th–8th June and in addition there are no twins on 7th June. It is fully booked for 4th and 5th July and there is a trade fair from 1st to 4th August. Most large hotels install charts similar to this in their reservation office and the information is updated as necessary by the reservations supervisor.

Key: ○ = no singles   ☐ high demand period
       □ = no twins
       △ = no suites

Fig. 3.11 Part of a stop-go chart

Control of reservations

CLOSE OUTS

A stop-go chart is an ideal method for the reservations supervisor to ensure maximum control of reservations.

The chart can be closed out by room type (i.e. no twins available on a particular date), or may be closed out by room type for arrivals only. This ensures that bookings will not be accepted for busy periods for one or two nights, but should an opportunity occur to secure a good booking, perhaps covering two weekends for example, it is possible to accept the reservation and 'book through' the busy period.

Alternatively the reservations supervisor may estimate that the hotel will be able to fill all its accommodation for a particular period, and so aim to control reservations by closing out reduced rate business, ensuring that maximum revenue is earned for that time.

OVERBOOKING

This is the practice of accepting more reservations than there is space available. The purpose of overbooking is to assist the hotel in obtaining maximum occupancy, and to compensate for early departures, last minute cancellations and non-arrivals. On the density chart (Fig. 3.8) overbooking was allowed to 25%. For most hotels this is a high figure. The reception department should keep figures of non-arrivals and early departures and from these should calculate the percentage to which overbooking is possible. In this way overbooking becomes a way of controlling reservations by booking to a pre-determined number of rooms based on the anticipated non-arrivals for that date. Viewed in this way overbooking becomes good sales technique, rather than sloppy and unprofessional practice.

The degree of overbooking will vary not only from one hotel to another but also from week to week and day to day in the same hotel.

Reservations Departments which are operating on a computer system will usually find that the system will record the relationship between reservations and actual arrivals, and even the likelihood of different classes of booking not arriving. Obviously this is a great boon to the hotel, and should ensure that serious overbooking never occurs.

A hotel with a highly transient trade will be able to overbook more than a hotel in a resort where guests book three months in advance and stay for two-week periods. The fact that a hotel overbooks does not mean that it will have to refuse guests rooms. The aim of overbooking is to balance exactly the extra rooms booked with the non-arrivals and cancellations. Only if this goes wrong is it necessary to 'book out' guests to another hotel. A middle way is to accept bookings on a waiting list for cancellations.

Confirming reservations

Many hotels send a letter of confirmation to people who make reservations. This serves a number of purposes. It can be evidence of a contract, and is obviously easier to prove than a verbal contract. The law is in favour of the person booking the room. A contract exists when the guest posts the letter of confirmation, and can only be cancelled by the hotel when the guest receives the letter withdrawing a previous offer. If the guest is not accommodated, then he or she may be able to sue for material loss as a result of the breaking of the contract. In certain states in the USA guests are able to sue for 'disturbance' if they are not accommodated by the hotel at which they booked.

REPLY-PAID POSTCARDS

Reply-paid postcards are given to guests by some hotels to encourage them to use the same hotel on return visits. These are addressed to the hotel, with no postage payable by the guest. They are printed with a booking request that allows guests to fill in the details of room type, arrival date, and number of nights, along with their name and signature. This is a contract in the normal way, but is sometimes qualified by the use of a '6 p.m. release' clause.

STANDARD LETTERS

As individual letters of confirmation become more expensive to type some hotels use a standard letter of confirmation to guests booking accommodation. With the use of window envelopes, these can cut down clerical time considerably. A development of this is the word processor, which prepares a letter with gaps for the clerk to enter the name of the guest and details of the booking. Standard letters on tape or disc can be prepared to cover the most common reservation requests, such as a quiet room, deposit, late arrival, garage space for car, and so on.

TELEX

Reservations made by telex are an automatic confirmation, and as such form a major section of the correspondence. It is most important to note, however, that a booking made on a public telex does not constitute a confirmation and care should be exercised when dealing with these bookings.

DEPOSITS

For some categories of guests, hotels ask for a deposit to be sent in advance. This is very common in resort hotels where guests may be asked to pay a non-returnable deposit when confirming the booking. Hotels also request deposits from people who will be arriving late, or from overseas visitors. A receipt is normally sent back with the confirmation. The details of the deposit are entered in the diary, and credited to the guest's account on arrival, or departure, according to the policy of the hotel. A deposit is useful if the reservations manager feels there may be some difficulty in claiming a charge for the non-arrival of the guest. It would be difficult, for example, to follow up a non-arrival charge to a guest from the other side of the world.

CANCELLATION

If a guest cancels the booking, then the reservation procedure has to be reversed; the booking is crossed through in the diary, the chart entry is erased and the details are married together in the files. The hotel may sue the guest for loss if the guest cancels the booking, but the hotel must make every attempt to re-let the accommodation, and can only claim for the actual loss incurred.

When a computerised system is in use a cancellation may continue to be displayed on the screen but be clearly marked as cancelled. This can be particularly useful in the case of amended arrival dates when it may be helpful to refer to previous information. If a guest cancels a booking for the week beginning 7th June and the hotel is able to re-let the accommodation for the last three nights of the week, a claim can only be made for the first four nights of the booking rather than the whole week. To claim for the whole week would be equal to selling the room twice.

While some seasonal hotels press claims for compensation when a guest cancels at short notice, it is very rare for city centre hotels to do so. Obviously this may vary if a tour cancels at very short notice, and the hotel has no chance of re-letting the accommodation, but this is normally covered by the terms of a special contract between the hotel and the tour operator.

NO CONFIRMATION

For a booking that is for the same day or in the next few days some hotels adopt the policy of not bothering to send a letter of confirmation, feeling that it will serve no purpose as the guest will already be resident by the time the confirmation arrives at his or her address. There is a risk, though, that the guest may not be known at the address booked from, so sending a confirmation, or even telephoning to confirm the booking can serve as a useful insurance policy. This is especially true if the guest has requested that the bill be sent to his or her company for payment.

Some large London 'transient' hotels have experimented with the policy of not sending any confirmations to guests at all, unless it is requested by the guest or an account booking. In this way they aim to minimise the cost of operating the reservation department.

FILING RESERVATIONS

All details of bookings and cancellations are stored in filing cabinets under the date of arrival of the guest. They may be organised in this file in alphabetical order, but the arrival date is considered to be the key piece of information. Letters are usually stapled together with the most recent letter or telex from the guest at the top of the file, in this way letters can be quickly retrieved from the files. By stapling letters together there is less chance of them becoming lost than if paper clips were used.

Status of reservations

6 P.M. RELEASE

Reservations are often taken on the basis that the guest will arrive by a certain time of day. If they arrive before that time they have their room in the normal way. If they arrive after the time they have to take a chance on a room being available when they arrive. This enables the hotel to be certain it is full, without the risk of having to charge guests for non-arrival if they are delayed or change their plans.

GUARANTEED ARRIVAL

This is the reverse of a 6 p.m. release. Here the guests guarantee to pay for the room whether they arrive or not. It is very useful for guests who may be arriving very late at night, or even early the next morning from a transatlantic flight. Guaranteed arrival facilities are normally offered only to companies, or travel agents, who the hotel can be certain will honour their commitment.

TAKE OR PLACE (T OR P)

Regular customers are often offered a 'take or place' booking if they reserve at short notice. When they arrive at the hotel a room will be allocated to them if there has been a cancellation. If there has not been any cancellation or non-arrival, then the hotel will find another room for them in a comparable hotel. This facility is often offered by chain hotels, for while one hotel in the group may be full, there may be vacancies elsewhere. This 'T or P' facility helps to retain customer loyalty and also maximises occupancy for individual hotels or groups.

VIPs AND CIPs

Reservations for Very Important Persons or Commercially Important Persons are normally handled by the senior reservations clerk to ensure that all arrangements are carried out correctly. Even in a hotel that operates with a density chart a room may be allocated at the time of booking for these guests. A note is normally made in the reservation diary, so that the duty manager will be informed when they arrive.

TOURS AND GROUPS

Each hotel will have its own definition of a tour, some specifying that any booking of more than five rooms shall be treated as a 'group'. Special procedures are generally followed for these reservations and any deposits that may be paid. These are explained fully in Chapter 8.

COMMISSIONABLE BOOKINGS

Reservations made by travel agents and hotel booking agents are normally subject to a commission payment to the agent on the room rate. This fact is noted in the remarks column of the diary, so that the bill can be marked as commissionable when the guest checks in. Frequently two bills may be opened—one for the apartment charge showing the appropriate commission, and a second bill for any extras incurred by the guest. This ensures that the commission is only deducted from the accommodation charge.

Self assessment questions

1 List the six methods by which a reservation may be communicated to a hotel.
2 Draw a specimen reservation form.
3 Explain three ways in which a conventional chart differs from a density chart.
4 What is the purpose of the reservation diary?
5 In what way is a rack system better than a diary?
6 What does a 'stop-go' chart do?
7 Explain what is meant by 'close-out'.
8 Briefly explain the following:
  (a) CIP
  (b) 6.00 p.m. release
  (c) T or P
  (d) commissionable.

Chapter 4

CHECK-IN AND GUEST IN HOUSE

Chapter objectives

After studying this chapter you should be able to:

- explain the systems and procedures required to ensure that a guest's reception and stay in the hotel meets legal requirements;
- explain the systems and procedures corresponding to organisational requirements.

Registration

There is a legal obligation for a hotel to obtain, and keep for twelve months, certain information about every person who stays there. The basic requirement is full name and nationality. If the guest is from overseas, then they have to provide in addition their passport number and place of issue, and their next destination and the address there, if known. A guest staying at a hotel need not in law provide their true name, but obviously the hotel would view with caution anyone they thought was not using their true name.

In addition to this legal minimum, hotels request further information from guests who stay with them. A home address and signature are asked for in all hotels. Others take the opportunity to find out more about their customers by asking for information such as car registration number, purpose of visit, occupation, proposed method of payment, and other details.

These requests can be placed into two categories; administrative, to ensure the smooth efficient running of the operation, and marketing, where the hotel takes the opportunity to find out more about its customers' habits.

REGISTER

The traditional method of checking guests in is to use a register. This is a large, bound book ruled into columns which the guest fills out upon arrival. It is ideal for smaller hotels where guests arrive individually. A register provides a permanent record of

47

Date	Family name	Other names	Full address	Signature	Room	Nationality
23/6	Sparrow	George	11 Field Lane Warmington	G. Sparrow	321	British
23/6	Finch	Clive	27, Fowlers Walk, Ealing	C. Finch	709	U.K.
23/6	Finch	Janet	27 Fowlers Walk Ealing W5	J. Finch	709	U.K.

Fig. 4.1 Specimen page of a register

guests staying in the hotel; it is unlikely to be lost, and guests are recorded in chronological order. The cost per guest is also very low, for each guest will take up only one line of the register. A typical register is shown in Fig. 4.1.

Overseas guests are normally asked to fill out a supplementary Aliens Form to provide the additional information that is required (*see* Fig. 4.2).

The register suffers from some disadvantages. If more than one guest wishes to check-in there is a waiting time; in the case of a tour this time could be considerable. Also, the receptionist is unable to process registration information while a guest is checking in, so administration delays could occur in notifying other departments, and opening the bill. As each guest individually registers, there may be entries made in the wrong column

---

OVERSEAS VISITORS

Family name _Corbeau_   Other names _Charles_

Passport no. _XY 12345_   Place of _Paris_
                             issue

Nationality _French_   Next destination _Oxford_

Date _23/6_

Fig. 4.2 Aliens form

which need to be crossed out. Handwriting and inks will differ, and the overall effect becomes rather untidy. More importantly, it is an indiscreet method in that it provides the opportunity to find out information about other people staying at the hotel.

REGISTRATION CARD

To overcome this problem, separate registration cards are now in widespread use (*see* Fig. 4.3). This card has the advantages of both discretion and neatness; if the card is incorrectly filled out then it is a simple matter to give the guest another. Registration cards are more expensive than a register, but the cost is still low compared with the benefits they offer. The only drawback is that a registration card is more likely to be lost or mislaid than a bulky register, but efficient procedures can guard against this.

The registration card can be modified to suit the needs of a particular hotel; for example motor hotels may require a car registration number, commercial hotels may require company affiliation and airport hotels may require details such as flight departure time.

To cut down costs some hotels have combined registration and reservation cards by printing them back to back (*see* Fig. 3.3). Group hotels can standardise registration cards by printing only the group name on them. This promotes a brand image, and also

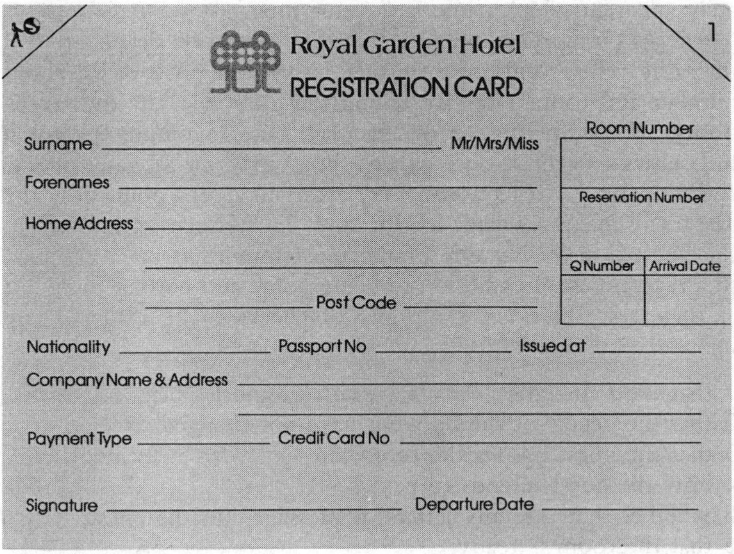

1

Royal Garden Hotel
REGISTRATION CARD

Room Number

Reservation Number

Q Number | Arrival Date

Surname ______ Mr/Mrs/Miss

Forenames ______

Home Address ______

______

______ Post Code ______

Nationality ______ Passport No ______ Issued at ______

Company Name & Address ______

______

Payment Type ______ Credit Card No ______

Signature ______ Departure Date ______

Fig. 4.3 Registration card

allows for printing economies through larger print orders. International hotels sometimes produce registration cards in a number of languages to help guests when they are checking in.

A computer system will usually include a facility to exempt a guest from constantly re-registering at a hotel. The system may automatically transfer booking details onto a registration document, or may be a storage system for those guests who have stayed in the hotel before. This means that on a return visit by a guest the computer will search the files and reproduce the registration details. Even in the most modern systems the guest is still usually asked to sign—without a signature it would be difficult to prove that charges had been incurred, and there would be no proof of the guest's stay. This is particularly important when the account is sent to a company for payment. A computer may also be programmed with details of any undesirable guests who may have caused problems in the past, or been 'blacklisted'.

CHECKING

The receptionist should always check the registration card or register once the guest has checked in. It is then possible to make sure that the card has been completed correctly and that the information is legible. If there is a query the receptionist can politely ask the guest for clarification and enter the details. This is particularly important with some nationalities where it is not immediately apparent which name is the surname.

It is also important to check that the reservation details are still the same. The receptionist can then inform the guest of the room number and room rate. By telling the guest the rate the receptionist is complying with the law and avoiding potential difficulties at check-out, when there may be a rate query. Additionally the receptionist may ascertain at this point how the guest will make payment for the stay. To summarise, registering the guest is probably one of the most important tasks assigned to a receptionist. In addition to being polite and putting the guest at their ease there are a number of checks to be made. These include:

1 that the registration details are correct and legible;
2 that the details of the booking have not changed;
3 that the guest knows the room rate and what it includes;
4 how the guest intends to pay;
5 whether there are any letters or messages for the guest;
6 that the room is ready;
7 that sales techniques have been used to maximum effect.

BOOKING OUT

The chapter on reservations explained the principle and aims of overbooking. When a mistake is made in the amount of overbooking, it is necessary to send some arrivals to another hotel, because there is no space for them. The first stage in handling the situation is to ensure that the arrival list is absolutely correct, that there are no entries that have been cancelled, or switched to another date or entered twice. The reception manager can then establish the exact number of guests it will be necessary to book out. At the same time a check can be made to ascertain the length of time the hotel is overbooked for; is it one night, two nights or longer? All arrivals due can be classified into six groups according to their booking source:

1 UK individuals;
2 overseas individuals;
3 UK companies;
4 overseas companies;
5 UK travel agents;
6 overseas travel agents.

From these groups should be removed all VIPs and CIPs who are to be given priority in room allocation. The residue will provide the people who can be booked out. The aim of the hotel in overbooking in the first place was to maximise income, so in booking out guests it is important to choose people who, if offended, have the least effect upon the business in the long term. Therefore, it is preferable to book out a guest from overseas who is unlikely to return, rather than a guest booked by the hotel's largest business house user.

Normally the hotel will reserve alternative accommodation for the guest in a hotel that is at least as good, and pay all the out of pocket expenses of the guest, taxi fares, telephone calls etc. If the hotel is in a group then if at all possible another group hotel is used. Telephone and other guest contact departments are notified of the hotel that the guest has been re-booked into: in this way all messages will be passed on as quickly as possible.

Any guest who is booked out will have a genuine grievance against the hotel, and will probably complain vehemently; for this reason the actual handling of the booking out is best done by the senior receptionist on duty, or the assistant manager.

CHANCE ARRIVALS

A guest who stays at the hotel without a prior booking is often

51

referred to as a 'chance' guest. 'Transient' hotels will receive the bulk of their guests as chance arrivals.

The receptionist has less information about the potential guest and their credit-worthiness in this situation, so special procedures are adopted to handle their bookings.

Chance arrivals with substantial amounts of luggage are unlikely to be able to leave the hotel without paying, for their departure would be noticed by a member of staff. An increasing trend, however, is the carrying of small amounts of luggage, which means the guest may be able to leave unnoticed. In registering the guest, the receptionist first checks whether they have luggage; if they do, then the registration is processed in the normal way and the registration card is marked 'Chance'.

If there is little or no luggage, then the receptionist has to ensure that the guest will not leave without first settling his or her bill. This can be done either by taking a cash deposit from the guest, or alternatively by taking an imprint of any credit card that the guest may have. Certainly in registering a chance guest it is essential that some corroboration of the details of the registration card is obtained. Obviously, it is important that in accepting chance bookings and taking deposits, the receptionist does not suggest to the guest that the hotel thinks they may be dishonest, or not willing to pay. Chance guests are often asked to pay cash for all purchases while they are in the hotel, or alternatively, a special check may be kept on the size of their bill, so that if the account exceeds a set figure (say £100) the guest is contacted and asked to pay up to that date. By doing this potential losses from chance guests are minimised.

NO TRACE RESERVATIONS

Even in the most efficient office there will be an occasion when a guest arrives to check in and there is no trace of the reservation. This can occur for a variety of reasons but the remedy is nearly always the same—the guest must be asked for details of the booking. This must be done as discreetly as possible and then all the records must be checked. The reservation may have been listed under the company name, or the name of the person who made the booking. It is also possible that the guest made two bookings at once, and one of them may have been overlooked, or has not been cross referenced.

After the correspondence has been checked and an exhaustive search made, normal arrival procedure should be adopted. Remember, if the client is unknown to you the booking should be treated as if it were chance—an excellent opportunity to demonstrate social skills.

KEY CARD

Some hotels give a key card to their guests when they check in. This is either a card or small booklet which has the guest's name, room number and room rate on it. Inside there are details of the restaurants and other hotel facilities. Often this is linked with

WELCOME TO THE

Royal Garden Hotel

Kensington High Street, London W8 4PT. 01-937 8000 Telex 263151 Cables ROYGARTEL London W8

Guest Name

Arrival Date   Departure Date

Room Number   Room Rate

(Rooms should be vacated by 12 noon on the day of departure)
IMPORTANT Please show this card each time you collect your key and when you sign charges to your room account.

ROYAL ROOF
RESTAURANT

Situated on the 10th floor, this luxurious restaurant
and cocktail bar offers superb views of London.
Diners may enjoy a choice of leisurely
breakfasts, excellent fixed price and à la carte
lunches and dinners with live music and dancing
in the evenings.

THE GARDEN CAFE
On the ground floor overlooking Kensington
Gardens, this bright Brasserie style restaurant
is open every day.

7 a.m. – 11 p.m.

Enjoy breakfast, lunch, dinner,
coffee and snacks

GARDEN BAR
Popular with both hotel guests and local residents
for many years. This bar with its garden view has
a lively atmosphere created by our resident
pianist.

GALLERY BAR
Overlooking the hotel lobby and bustling
Kensington High Street, this is the place to meet.
It offers a superb range of champagnes and
international beers.

ROOM SERVICE
A 24 hour facility for snacks, full meals and
beverages is available by telephoning
extension 44.

Fig. 4.4 Key card

53

advertising for local shops and services and may then be self-financing. Key cards can be printed in different colours to indicate the different status of guests. A red key card, for example, would identify a chance guest, who would then be asked to pay cash for all house purchases. A key card fulfils three separate functions:

1 it can be used as a security check when guests collect their keys;
2 it advertises facilities both in and out of the hotel;
3 it satisfies the obligation to inform guests of their room rate when they register. This is shown in Fig. 4.4.

KEYS

The key card is given to the guest by the receptionist and shows that the check in procedure is almost complete.

The key itself may not be kept at reception since in the larger hotels it will almost certainly be held by the porters or at the information desk. Keys are usually kept on a large tag to prevent clients from taking them away (either intentionally or by accident). The tag is usually marked with the room number and the name of the hotel to facilitate return should it be taken away, and is consequently a big security problem.

ELECTRONIC KEYS

Replacing the common system of keys, sub-master keys and master keys for hotel rooms is a new system of electronic keys. These are plastic credit card type keys which are printed for each new arrival with a fresh combination number. Sub-master and master keys follow the same format. If a key is lost or stolen it is a simple task to reprogram all the locks. Hotel security is consequently improved. These keys can also be used for authorisation and direct debiting in the restaurant, bar, and other sales areas of the hotel. This eliminates the risk of charges being posted to the wrong room. Linked with a cash register that has preset pricing for each item the system becomes virtually foolproof.

Room status

A prime need for every hotel is an accurate, up-to-date knowledge of the state of every room in the hotel. A room can be in one of four states:

1 let;
2 vacant and not ready;

3 vacant and ready;

4 closed for repair or decoration.

A room status system must be able to show these four positions and be capable of being quickly changed. Systems adopted range from the very simple manual system that will operate in a small hotel to computerised systems that carry out a number of management functions in large city centre hotels.

BEDROOM BOOK

This is the most basic system. It is operated completely manually and requires a large amount of clerical work. But, because it is generally used in hotels of less than 20 rooms, this is not too demanding.

The bedroom book is normally a diary that has a page for each day. A line is ruled for each day, for every room in the hotel. As the guest registers, their name is written next to the room number on the page of the arrival day, and is rewritten for each day that they stay. So, if a guest books for fourteen nights, their name is written on fourteen pages of the bedroom book. From Fig. 4.5 it can be seen that room 10 is occupied by Mr and Mrs J Finch on 10th and 11th June, and they are paying a rate of £15 per night.

Next to room numbers are the room types. Room 12 is occupied by Mr H Sparrow on 10th, but he is due to check out on 11th. There has to be a method of showing that a room has been occupied overnight, or a receptionist may send an arrival to room 12 before the guest has left, or before it is ready. A common way

Monday 10th June		Tuesday 11th June	
10 T Finch, Mr/s. J.	£15	10 T Finch, Mr/s. J.	£15
11 TB		11 TB	
12 S Sparrow, Mr. H.	£8	12 S	
14 D		14 D	
15 DB		15 DB	

Fig. 4.5 Entries in bedroom book

of doing this is to use three sides of a triangle to show the state of the room. So:

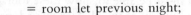

/   = room let previous night;

\/   = room vacant but not ready;

▽   = room vacant and ready to re-let.

As with the reservation chart, if guests leave early or extend their stay the receptionist has to update the bedroom book accordingly. This applies to all the room status systems. Individual hotels modify this system to their own needs in many different ways, but in all cases it has the advantage of providing a permanent record of room status. Fig. 4.5 also shows that the room numbers are 10, 11, 12, 14, 15. There is no room 13. Many hotels avoid numbering a room 13, to avoid incidents with superstitious guests. This is also the case in larger hotels, where there is rarely a floor numbered 13.

BED SHEET

The bed sheet or room letting sheet is a development of the bedroom book and is often used in hotels of up to 200 rooms. The information is recorded onto a sheet pre-printed with room numbers, types and three sections. One sheet is used for each day and the day and date are entered by the receptionist. During the evening shift, the entries are copied over onto the sheet of the next day.

Figure 4.6 shows the three section bed sheet for 11th June. Guests are entered into the appropriate column depending on whether they are arriving, staying or leaving. A guest who was booked for only one night would move straight from the arrivals column to the departures. This three-column system is very effective, for it enables the receptionist to see quickly the rooms that will be available to let that day. It is also possible to allocate rooms before guests have checked out.

In the example (*see* Fig. 4.6) of 11th June, it can be seen that Mr Dove in Room 102 is staying until 20th June. Room 103 is being vacated by Mr and Mrs Jay, and the receptionist has allocated the room to Mr and Mrs Raven. In completing the sheet, the receptionist would write the room allocations in pencil, so that

Day _Tuesday_   Date _11th June_

Room	Arrivals				Staying				Departures			
	Name	Sleepers	Rate	Dep.	Name	Sleepers	Rate	Dep.	Name	Sleepers	Rate	Dep.
101 TB												
102 SB					Dove	1	£20	20/6				
103 D	Raven	2	£30	13/6					Jay	2	£30	11/6
104 TRB												
105 DB												
106 S	↓				←— Off for re-decoration —→							

Fig. 4.6 Part of bed sheet

57

changes can be easily made. When the guests arrive and have registered, then the details can be entered in ink in the arrival column. During the evening shift the receptionist will copy over the details of each room from the sheet of one day to the new sheet. Thus in the example, Mr and Mrs Raven would be entered into the 'staying' column of the bed sheet of 12th June. It is still necessary to show whether or not the departure has been made, and also whether or not the room has been cleaned and returned by the housekeeping department.

ROOM BOARD

A room board is used in larger hotels. The board is made of slots located next to each room number. As each guest registers, a small card is filled out with details of the guest and the length of stay and this is placed into the appropriate room slot. When the guest checks out, the card is removed and thrown away. With this system, there is much less clerical work, for the guest's name is written only once. Coloured cards can be used to show whether or not a room is ready to be occupied. A room board is a quick, visual guide to room status, but unlike the previous two systems, it does not provide a permanent record (*see* Fig. 4.7).

ROOM STATUS BOARDS (e.g. Whitney)

A room status system is simply a development of the room board. Although some of the components are interchangeable with the

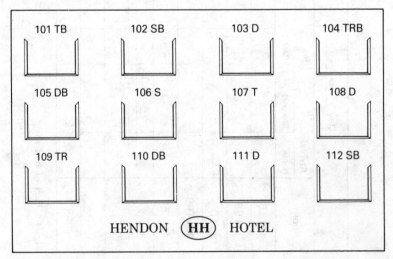

Fig. 4.7 Part of room board

advance reservation rack system, they do not have to be used together. There is a rack for all the rooms of the hotel with a slot for each room. The rack is tailor-made for each hotel. In some systems there is a perspex slider which can be in one of three positions relating to the colours clear, red or yellow. The room type is shown in the centre of each slot, and the room types are colour coded over the room numbers on the left. In this way, the room type can be identified even when a rack slip is in place. Arrows are used to show communicating rooms. The centre section can also be used to show the room rate and the location of each room.

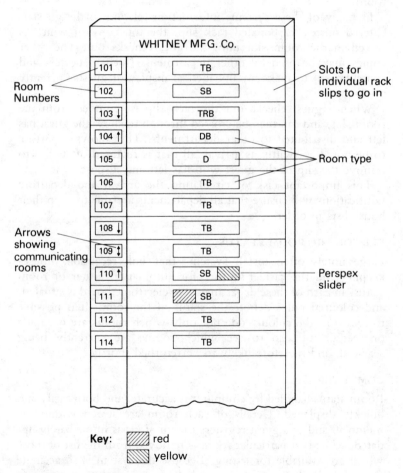

Key: ▨ red
     ▧ yellow

Fig. 4.8 Part of room status rack

With this method, the maximum information about the room is presented to the receptionist.

The three colours of the perspex slider can be used to show the current state of the room (*see* Fig. 4.8):

1 red   = room vacant but not ready;
2 clear   = room vacant and ready;
3 yellow = room just let.

The advantage of a room status board such as this is that more than one receptionist can register guests and allocate rooms instantly, minimising the risk of two people being given the same room.

In many of these systems information relating to the guest is entered onto a carbonated rack slip, the top copy of which is placed in the room slot until the guest checks out. The other copies may be used by other departments (such as porters and switchboard) to make an alphabetical display of guests currently in the hotel.

When a guest checks out the rack slip is removed from the room slot, and can then be crossed through to show the guest has left and distributed to other departments. This allows departure to be noted as swiftly as arrival; all that is required of staff is to remove the slip of the guest who has left and dispose of it.

This important task of circulating the arrival and departure notifications will ensure that all departments are able to keep their house lists in order.

ELECTRONIC ROOM STATUS

Large hotels often install systems that link reception, house-keeping and the cashier's office for automatic transfer of room status. In each of these departments an electronic board is situated, and coloured bulbs denote the status of the room. It is possible to see from the colour code not only which rooms are occupied or ready, but also to see which rooms are currently being serviced, and therefore likely to be returned shortly.

COMPUTER

Room status handled by computer is accurate, and both easily and quickly displayed. Details of each room are stored within the memory, and as a guest registers the guest list is immediately updated, while that particular room is removed from the list of those which are available for letting. Because the system is so accurate there is little chance of two people being given the same room.

ROOM ALLOCATION

When the guests arrive they will want to be able to use their rooms as quickly as possible. If they arrive before midday, then it is unlikely that the rooms will be ready unless they are vacant from the previous night. In smaller hotels allocation of rooms is normally done at the time of booking, by using the conventional chart. If when a guest arrives the room allocated is not ready, but a similar one is, then the chart has to be changed round to show the re-allocation. Larger hotels with a greater choice of rooms often do not allocate until the guest actually arrives, and then place the guest in the room of the type required that is ready. VIPs and guests with special requirements may have rooms pre-allocated to them and a note may be placed in the reception area to ensure that they only go to those particular rooms. In allocating rooms the receptionist should aim to satisfy the guests as much as possible. Even in large modern hotels not every room is exactly the same, some may have better views than others, and certain rooms may be particularly noisy due to their proximity to the lift or a service pantry. Allocation should take place on the basis of putting the guests who are staying the longest into the best rooms at their rate, and guests who booked first into rooms better than those guests who booked at the last moment or are chance arrivals. By following this strategy the rooms in the hotel that are the least satisfactory will always be the last to be let. Out of season some hotels let only sections of the hotel so that whole floors may be closed down, either for cleaning, or to save unnecessary lighting and heat.

A hotel which operates a computerised system will ensure that the program carries provision for different tariffs, locations and individual guest preferences. The computer will select the best available room for a particular reservation, or offer alternatives if the preferred room is already taken or not yet ready. It is essential that the program is flexible enough to ensure that any special requests by guests can be catered for.

Notifications and records

A system of departmental notifications and records has to be kept to ensure that the needs of the guest (and management) are satisfied. In a hotel where a computer is in use these notifications and records pose no problem at all.

A sensible method of distribution would be to ensure the placing of a VDU in all relevent departments. This would enable the arrival and departure situation to be updated instantly, and room changes recorded without tedious paper work. Additionally the other departments could request information from the computer if required, and save themselves time and trouble.

Many hotels, however, still rely on traditional methods of notifications to other departments.

ARRIVAL LIST

Normally one day in advance an alphabetical arrival list is prepared showing all guests due to arrive, their length of stay and any special requirements they may have. This list will be useful to both the porter and the telephonist. The porter or enquiry desk

REMOVAL SLIP -   RECEPTION

Name ....

From Room No. ....

To Room No. ....

Group Name ....

No. PERSONS

From ....   To ....

RATE CHANGE

From ....   To ....

Remarks:

Date ....   Time ....

Signature ....

                                        Reception.

AH52

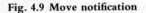

— Housekeeper
— Switchboard
— Porters

Fig. 4.9 Move notification

will wish to check if there are any messages or letters for guests arriving and the telephonist may answer enquiries from people about the arrival of particular guests. Tour members or conference delegates are normally listed separately under the name of the booking agent. The reception desk will be able to use the alphabetical list to locate guests quickly in the diary.

DEPARTMENTAL NOTIFICATIONS

Individual arrival notifications are rarely used now, although a rack slip serves the same purpose. When a tour has arrived, and the rooms have been allocated, a tour list is passed to each department as soon as possible so that queries can be answered.

Moves from one room to another require an individual notification because the records of each department need to be updated. A typical move notification is shown in Fig. 4.9.

HOUSE LIST

An alphabetical guest list is usually prepared each evening by the reception department. This is then distributed throughout the hotel, though some departments may only check it occasionally. The telephone department, porter's desk and recepiton will need to refer to it constantly, but there is little need for the kitchen to receive one. A list of guests in room number order is only kept at the reception through the room board, or bed sheet, and anyone wishing to know who is in a particular room would have to check with the reception desk. For many 'transient' hotels the house list is only an approximation for as soon as it is distributed the position has been changed by the departure of some guests and the arrival of others.

DEPARTURE LIST

The departure list is prepared in room number order and is often combined with the house list for circulation to all departments of the hotel. Work allocation by the housekeeping department will be done from the departure list.

FUNCTION/TOUR LIST/TEN-DAY FORECAST

All the previous lists and notifications are prepared daily. Once a week the reception department will distribute a list of functions and tours that are booked for the following ten days. This list assists the planning of staffing levels over the period, and ensures that staff are aware of projected levels of occupancy in the week to come.

CALL/PAPERS/EMT

The reception department may keep a sheet at the front desk which records the exact time at which guests wish to be called in the morning, their newspaper order and requests for early morning tea or breakfast (*see* Fig. 4.10). Increasing use is being made of semi-automatic equipment in this area to relieve the pressure on staff during the morning peak. Some hotels are installing alarm clocks in guest rooms, along with tea-making equipment. Breakfast order forms are also placed in the room for the guest to complete and hang outside the door at night.

	Room	Paper	E.M.T.		Room	Paper	E.M.T.		Room	Paper	E.M.T.
7.00				7.45				8.30			
7.15	310	Guardian	1	8.00	207	Times	2	8.45			
7.30	709	Sun	–	8.15				9.00			

Fig. 4.10 Part of early call newspapers and early morning tea sheet

Name Sparrow, Mr. George					
Address 11 Field Lane, Warmington			Tel. 051. 235. 1234.		
Remarks Likes high room. A/C to Birds Ltd.					
Arrival	Departure	Room	Rate	Bill total	
14/5	15/5	723	£20	56.70.	

Fig. 4.11 Guest history card

GUEST HISTORY CARDS

Luxury hotels have always used guest history cards to record details of each individual stay by guests, and information on their personal likes and dislikes. 'Transient' hotels have less need of this, due to the short average stay of the guest, the uniformity

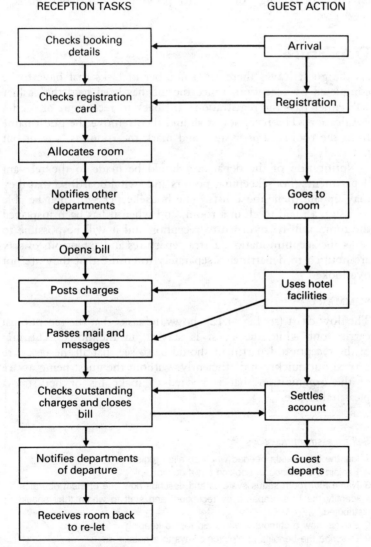

Fig. 4.12 Flowchart of guest stay

of hotel facilities and the fact that the guest is unlikely to make a return visit. The cost of keeping a guest history system up-to-date is thought by many hotels to outweigh the benefits. This can be alleviated by the use of a modified system for regular visitors to the hotel (*see* Fig. 4.11) or ensuring that it is part of a computer reservation program, when it can be easily analysed for more effective marketing, or used to provide a more personalised service.

Departure

As the guest leaves there are a number of tasks that have to be completed by reception. Once the bill has been paid the cashier will either pass the registration card back to reception, or send a notification. The receptionist should then remove the guest name from the room status system and mark the room as 'vacant but not ready'.

Notification of the departure should be made to the relevant departments (housekeeping, porters and switchboard) so that they may update their house lists. The housekeeper will then be able to assign a maid to clean a room, and when it has been inspected the room will be returned to reception and it will be possible to re-let the accommodation. Extra departures and extensions of stay are notified to departments separately to ensure that they are not overlooked.

SUMMARY

The flow chart (*see* Fig. 4.12) shows the tasks that the receptionist carries out while the guest is staying in the hotel. The aim of the reception department should be to see that all the tasks are carried out quickly and efficiently, without the guest being aware of the organisation that is needed to make his or her stay a pleasurable one.

Self assessment questions

1 List the information needed when an alien registers.
2 Explain the method of booking out a guest.
3 Name four room status systems and describe how one of them operates.
4 Identify the lists prepared by reception, and staff to whom they should be distributed.
5 Explain how a computer would aid record keeping.
6 Describe the benefits of electronic keys to a hotel.

Chapter 5

COMMUNICATIONS AND OFFICE PRACTICE

Chapter objectives

After studying this chapter you should be able to:

- explain what is meant by non verbal communication;
- describe how verbal communication will differ when dealing with different types of people;
- list the main occasions when internal written communication will be in use;
- explain the recent advances in telecommunications.

Communication plays a vital part in any business, but most especially in hotels.

In some form or another communication figures in every aspect of the work of a hotel receptionist, and the information which plays such an important part of the work can be transmitted in various ways. Communication may be:

1 non verbal
2 verbal
3 written
4 telecommunications

Non verbal communication

This describes all the silent ways in which you display your feelings. Non verbal communication is conveyed in your facial expression, which can show a welcoming smile or a forbidding frown. Most of us are aware that we have 'good' days and 'bad' days, but in reception they must all *appear*, at least, to be good days.

A favourable and welcoming expression can be readily created by observing several elementary non verbal aspects of behaviour.

NEAT APPEARANCE

Essential at all times in front office, as an individual neatly presented gives the impression of a well organised and well run department. Imagine how quickly you would become disillusioned if you went for an interview for a job and the personnel manager had a stained blouse or dirty fingernails.

PERSONAL HYGIENE

A very basic aspect of non verbal communication, but one which cannot be over emphasised. Remember that an important front office task is selling accommodation, and reception staff are frequently required to show guests to rooms. The guest will not be impressed if the atmosphere in the lift is unpleasant, and the sale may well be lost.

POSTURE

Both sitting and standing posture should be carefully attended to. Not only will the correct posture make you less tired at the end of the day but it can easily reflect efficiency and enthusiasm, or show disenchantment.

The whole attitude of an individual is frequently portrayed by the way in which they stand—postures adopted can show shyness, reluctance, aggressiveness, willingness and many others.

Be sure to display an upright stance with arms unfolded—a confident yet welcoming posture.

EYE CONTACT

Use of correct eye contact is one of the vital skills which is essential to any 'people' industry. It is the non verbal equivalent of using someone's name. It establishes a personal contact, and warmth and humour are only two important emotions which can be expressed through eye contact. It is most disconcerting having a conversation with someone who refuses to meet your eyes, and many people assume that one who avoids eye contact is untrustworthy. In fact it more frequently suggests insecurity or shyness, neither one of them an attribute to associate with front office work.

Verbal communication

Good verbal communication is essential in most jobs but rarely does it play such an important part as in the reception office.

Most hotels place a good deal of importance upon the way in which their hotel receptionists speak. Because of the nature of the work it is important to use a clear and well modulated tone, pronouncing words clearly and never dropping the first or last letters of words.

Most hotels are dealing with a national, or international client-ele, and so accurate pronounciation is essential. Many overseas visitors may understand only a little English, and so strong regional accents can pose a problem.

While it is without doubt essential to speak clearly and without ambiguity to ensure effectiveness many people in fact omit the most important aspect of communicating—the art of listening.

If the reception staff are unable to listen properly the wrong information could be communicated—often with disastrous results. The reception office of a hotel could be compared to a clearing house in banking. The information arrives, is sorted, and then redirected to the appropriate place. Often reception are dependent upon other departments to send them information, but once received it is the responsibility of reception to ensure that all other sections are made aware of any changes or new devel-opments (*see* Fig. 5.1).

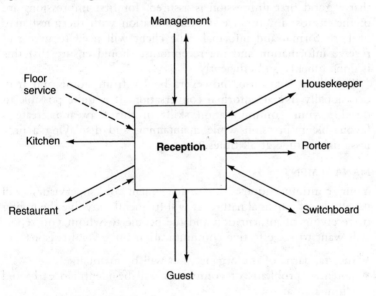

Fig. 5.1 Reception as the clearing house

If you cannot rely upon your memory, take notes, or identify and highlight the important points. If you are unsure about some-thing check or question the information which you have received. Above all listen, and act upon what you have heard. There are some people who ask questions and then do not listen to the answer. This is not only pointless but very rude. Be interested, listen to the communication which is directed to you.

The receptionist is expected to be able to deal with many different types of people, some of whom will require special treatment. Those who are deaf or hard of hearing will understand perfectly providing communication is properly carried out. There is no need to shout, but clear speech, slightly louder than usual, should prove effective. It is important to face the client and ensure that diction is clear.

It is particularly important in reception to develop the skill of communications at all levels. The reception staff are the buffer between management, guest and other staff, and communication skills will be required when dealing with all groups of people.

THE GUEST

The receptionist must communicate with the guest in such a way that a good first impression is assured, for first impressions are of the utmost importance. Communication with the guest may be both formal and informal. The client will need to give and receive information and the receptionist should ensure that this is done quickly and efficiently.

The client may also, however, be far from home and may occasionally like an informal conversation. It is quite possible to develop your communication skills in this way and create a favourable impression while maintaining and displaying a professional attitude at all times.

MANAGEMENT

Your communication with management or supervisors will usually be of a formal nature. It will frequently involve the giving or receiving of information and the people to whom you report will want to see effective communication for several reasons.

- the standards of the organisation will be maintained;
- potential problems or complaints will be identified early and eliminated at source;
- poor communications often leads to disillusionment and lack of motivation which may result in unnecessary staff turnover.

PEERS

Communications with your contemporaries will be different again, in that while they may be formal in content, (e.g. advising the housekeeper of moves, enquiring about baggage from the porters) it will be informal communication in that you are all on a similar level. The way in which you communicate with your peers reflects ultimately upon the smooth running of the hotel. Inevitably there will be occasional clashes of personality but these should never be allowed to develop to the stage where they are detrimental to the hotel. A negative attitude affects an entire shift, and everyone very quickly becomes unsettled. The hotel business is first and foremost about people, and that means enjoying the company of all types: young, old, either sex and all nationalities. The ability to work as part of a team cannot be overemphasised—an individual who can do the work but is a 'loner' has no future in front office.

Written communication

Written communication forms a major part of the work of the reception office. It may be handwritten, typewritten or transmitted by telex or computer but certainly most important information will be confirmed in a permanent way.

Basically the written communication and documentation in front office may be divided into two categories:

1 Internal
2 External

INTERNAL

Internal communication may often be informal and brief: the housekeeper notifying reception of ready rooms or the reception staff notifying other departments of an arrival. Regardless of their apparent informality this form of communication is vital and must be legible, with accurate and unambiguous information. Communications of this nature must also be distributed with all speed to ensure that each department is in possession of up-to-date information.

Documents in common use for internal communication are many and varied but could include some of the following:

● memos
● arrival and departure lists
● arrival and departure notifications
● guest in house lists
● tour rooming lists
● function lists

Other in-house communication systems in common use include:

71

- pocket paging—'Bleeps'—an electronic radio device small enough to carry in the pocket, activated by the switchboard operator to call senior staff to the telephone
- public address system—useful for paging guests and staff, but must be used with discretion
- Intercoms—internal telephones for use between offices, and occasionally sister hotels
- in-house TV promotion—to advertise the hotel's facilities

EXTERNAL

For many potential guests the written communication which they receive from a hotel may be their first contact with the establishment.

A letter which is badly written or typed, with incorrect spelling, gives a very bad impression and many guests will equate the standard of letter writing with the service provided by the hotel.

If the communication is hand written it must be clear and legible. If it is typewritten it must be accurate, without errors and following the correct format. The information which is conveyed should be up-to-date and without ambiguity. Many hotels have adopted a standard or form letter for confirmations (*see* Fig. 5.2). This eliminates repetitive typing and ensures that all relevant information is included. Some hotels no longer send confirmations, preferring instead to rely upon a release system or communications by computer/telex.

Documents in common use for external communciation may include the following:

- letters
- invoices
- standard confirmations
- requests for payment

Telecommunication

TELEPHONE

No reference to communications would be complete without considering the vital role which the telephone plays in any business operation.

Effective communication by telephone will not only assist in selling the hotel, but will also promote an image of efficiency.

The rules which apply to good verbal communication are even

NORFOLK TOWERS HOTEL

34 NORFOLK PLACE LONDON W2 1QW
Telephone: 01-262 3123 Telex: 268583 NORTOW

CONFIRMATION OF RESERVATION

Your Ref: ....

Our Ref: ....

Date ....

We have pleasure in confirming/offering you the following reservations:

Date of Arrival	No. of Nights	Name/s	Room	Daily Rate	Remarks

DAILY RATE: Inclusive of Continental Breakfast and Service Charge but exclusive of Value Added Tax.
RESERVATIONS: Accommodation will be automatically released at 15.00 hours unless a deposit has been received or arrival is guaranteed by Company.
DEPOSITS: The first night's charges are required in advance as a holding deposit along with your letter of confirmation.
ON ARRIVAL: Rooms may not be available before mid-day.
ON DEPARTURE: Rooms should be vacated by mid-day.
PERSONAL CHEQUES: We regret that personal cheques can be accepted only if prior arrangements have been made or on production of your Banker's Cheque Card provided your account is within the limits set by the card.
We regret it has become necessary to pay for all accommodation in advance on arrival. We apologise for any inconvenience.
We reserve the right to provide alternative accommodation and services of higher or similar standard. Rates shown on this confirmation are subject to alteration, without prior notice, only when Government Taxes are changed.
Should you require further information regarding this reservation please contact the hotel directly.
Assuring you of our best attention at all times.

ROOM CODE:
S : Single
SB : Single/Bath
SS : Single/Shower
T : Twin
TB : Twin/Bath
TS : Twin/Shower
D : Double
DB : Double/Bath
DS : Double/Shower
TR : Triple
TRB : Triple/Bath
TRS : Triple/Shower
S/occ : Single Occupancy

Fig. 5.2 Form letter

more applicable to telephone communication since the client has only the telephone conversation on which to judge the standard of the hotel.

Many hotels insist upon their staff answering the telephone in a certain way, e.g. 'Good morning, The Cross Hotel, Marie speaking, how may I help you?' This quickly becomes standard procedure and ensures that the client receives all the information.

As long as the call is answered promptly with an appropriate greeting the client will feel confident that the organisation is efficient. In addition to the correct greeting all switchboard

73

operators should be familiar with the procedure for overcoming the most common problems which occur:

- unobtainable numbers
- engaged numbers
- disconnected calls
- emergency calls

Most modern telephone systems enable the guest to dial direct both local and long distance calls. Help is available through the operator should the guest require assistance, and a range of other services will usually be provided by the switchboard operators:

- credit card calls
- ADC calls
- Directory Enquiries
- General enquiries
- Collect/reverse charge calls
- Early morning calls

Direct dialling

In most hotels when direct dialling from guest's rooms was introduced individual meters for each extention were installed in reception. This enabled the staff to calculate the number of units consumed, cost them according to the charge made by the hotel, and subsequently post the price to the guests account.

Unfortunately the system is not without problems since staff occasionally forget to read the meters, and so those units may be added to the bill of an incoming client.

Should a client dispute a charge it is almost impossible to check the cost of the call, and much revenue can be lost in this way.

Computerised phone billing

A computerised switchboard enables the billing of telephone calls to be controlled as never before. Each call is logged with the date and exact time, the number which was called, how long the call was connected for, the number of units consumed and then the cost of the call according to the hotel's charges. This can then be automatically charged to the guest's account, or printed out for the guest to see in case of query, or used for control purposes (*see* Fig. 5.3). The advantages of the system are two-fold.

1 The client cannot dispute the call, and billing is instantaneous and so revenue is unlikely to be lost.
2 Telephone logging systems of this type can also be fitted to any

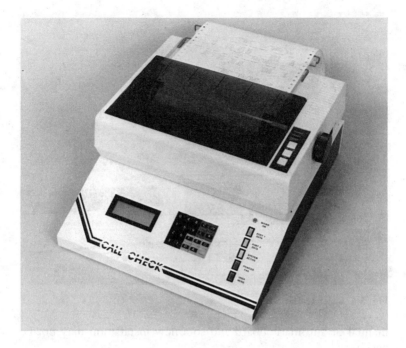

Fig. 5.3 Call check and print out

Fig. 5.4 Tiger traffic

manual or automatic board and so a new installation may not be necessary.

Another useful attribute of this system is the facility of extension barring, either internal, local or long distance. This enables the hotel to control the use of individual telephones and limit them, for example, to local calls only. The system also deters administrative staff from making personal calls, or unnecessary or badly timed long distance calls. Since each communication is automatically recorded the management can ensure, by carefully monitoring the computer printout, that telephone communication is used effectively to maximise revenue at minimum cost.

The TIGER Traffic is a good example of a system providing a very effective management aid (*see* Fig. 5.4). The reports are many and varied but include:

- calls collated by extension
- calls to specific numbers
- departmental analysis
- billing details

Telex
A large number of hotel bookings are received by telex, and since

76

the machine may be left unattended and still receive messages the hotel need never lose a sale. Telex is charged in units according to time and distance and so most messages are transmitted after they have been pre-recorded on a tape. The tape is transmitted much faster than anyone could possibly type and so the costs are significantly reduced. The only disadvantage of communication by telex is that the correspondent at the other end must also be a subscriber—most organisations realise that the telex has a vital role to play and so this is rarely a problem.

British Telecom have recently introduced the Puma which is a word processing telex. It has a microprocessor memory, auto-

Fig. 5.5 The Puma telex machine

matic dialling and a built in directory enabling regular numbers to be called without referring to a list. Should the number you are calling be engaged the machine will simply store the message and transmit it when the machine at the other end becomes free.

A similar machine is the Cheetah, and like the Puma it too has the ability to automatically call numbers which are in frequent use. Most major manufacturers are now looking towards these big improvements which will assure the continued and increased use of telex in business and commerce.

Fax

Facsimile printing is simply a way of transmitting a document in its original form from one place to another. Because of this inaccuracies due to transcription errors are eliminated and diagrams and illustrations can be reproduced and received in their exact format. The two machines are linked together by a British Telecom line. The best description is one of two photocopiers joined by telephone. Most fax machines are now of the desk top variety and consequently small enough to install almost anywhere (*see* Fig. 5.6).

Documents, deeds and other information can be sent automatically 24 hours a day and messages can be timed to the exact

Fig. 5.6 Canon fax machine

second. Many models feature a delayed transmission with automatic dialling and re-dialling if necessary. This has the dual advantage of overcoming different time zones and also means that messages can be scheduled to be sent when call rates are at their very lowest.

Most machines transmit and receive up to A4 size, although some will accept larger documents.

These machines are rapidly becoming invaluable, not only to the hotel, but also to the many business people staying in the hotel who will gladly pay to use the facility.

Office practice

The tasks performed in the reception office are in many ways little different to those in any other office.

The skills most frequently required will include the following:

1 Typing/word processing
2 Filing
3 Duplicating

TYPING/WORD PROCESSING

Much of the typewritten communication will be internal, but letters which are being sent to a prospective client will only result in a sale if they are arranged in a professional manner with the correct form of address.

FILING

The main methods of filing in the reception are usually;

● alphabetical
● numerical

Guest accounts are usually filed in room number order (numerical) while registration cards may be filed alphabetically under the name of the client, or numerically under the room number of the guest.

Other methods of filing in common use include:

● chronological
● by subject

Confirmation letters are filed under the date of arrival (chronological) and then under the name of the guest (alphabetical).

Some function and conference business may be filed by subject (e.g. W—Weddings), while others will be filed under the name of the company making the reservation.

DUPLICATING

The staff in most reception offices will need to circulate information to other departments. If there are no more than a few copies required (e.g. a memo) a photocopy is often sufficient. On the occasions when a large number of copies may be required they are more likely to be made by spirit or ink duplicator.

ADDITIONAL TASKS

Postal services

Particularly in a small hotel where there is no separate enquiry office the reception staff will need to be conversant with the various postal services available to the hotel. The services most likely to be utilised by both hotel and guest include the following:

- recorded delivery
- registered post
- Datapost
- business reply service
- electronic mail

The receptionist should also be familiar with the various communication services such as Red Star and private courier services.

The hotel mail will frequently be the responsibility of the reception staff and this includes both incoming and outgoing mail for the hotel, the guests and the staff. Outgoing mail is frequently stamped through a franking machine since this reduces potential pilferage of postage stamps, enables the hotel to keep a check on outgoing mail and also allows for an advertising slogan to be printed.

Reference sources

Even when there is a separate enquiry office many guests will still go to reception for advice. The reception office should be well stocked with reference books to enable guests' enquiries to be dealt with efficiently. The material which should be available would normally include the following:

- local maps and guides
- information relating to local/national events

- timetables
- postal guides

Self assessment questions

1 List the main methods of non verbal communication.
2 Differentiate between different type of verbal communication.
3 Explain the use of telephone communications in front office.
4 Describe the use of telex and fax in front office.
5 Describe the main office skills required by the receptionist.

Chapter 6
BILLING

Chapter objectives
After studying this chapter you should be able to:
- identify the principles of billing guests for charges;
- examine the methods of preparing guest bills.

Principles of hotel billing

Every hotel needs to record the income it receives for selling its goods and services. At the simplest level this will be a cash register in each department and a central cash book showing all the income. Most hotels, however, allow guests to charge purchases to their account and pay the total on departure. Any system of recording charges should satisfy the following requirements:

1 Guest bills should be kept up-to-date.
2 Sales of different departments should be identifiable.
3 Balancing should be possible.
4 Control checks can be carried out.
5 It should be easy to operate.
6 It should be economical in time and money.

GUEST BILLS SHOULD BE KEPT UP-TO-DATE

Because hotels operate throughout 24 hours, guests may incur charges at any time of the day or night, and it should be possible for them to know what their total bill is at any time, so posting to bills should be carried out regularly throughout the day. It is essential that charges are quickly transferred from the sales points in the hotel to the bill office or some charges may be lost to the establishment. The smallest hotels may have to rely on staff to take charge vouchers by hand, while some hotels were built with a pneumatic tube system sending vouchers from the point of sale to the bill office by metal carriers. By far the quickest and most efficient system is to install a computer terminal at each point of sale and so information regarding charges can be transferred directly to the main computer in the bill office.

The busiest time of day in the bill and cash office is the morning, when guests are checking out. It is vital that charges are transferred and posted quickly during this period so that they are charged to guests before they depart. Hotels that charge separately for breakfast must have very efficient methods to post charges at this time, or revenue may be lost. For this reason, some hotels include breakfast charges with the apartment rate, which is charged in advance.

SALES OF DIFFERENT DEPARTMENTS SHOULD BE IDENTIFIABLE

The charges incurred must be clear to the guest, and also to the hotel. If the tariff is inclusive, then there will only be a daily charge on the guest's bill, but the hotel will require some breakdown of charges for control purposes.

The standard system of hotel accounting allows for the identification of sales and cost centres. Even the smallest hotel will wish to have a system of billing that can identify the spending of guests on lunch and dinner, and possibly they will wish to divide it further into the amounts spent on food and drink during these meals.

In many smaller hotels it is the function of the front office staff to perform the duties of Restaurant cashiering, although the sophistication of the operation in the larger establishments has ensured that it is a specialised task. Most systems will at least provide a duplicate bill, with a clear final total, and allow for some method of analysis regarding the final method of payment and the volume of the business done.

In setting up the system of billing it is important to provide enough information for the management, without producing so much that nothing at all can be done with it.

BALANCING IS POSSIBLE

Wherever cash or charges are recorded it is essential that a balance can be derived. The total of charges incurred should always match the accounts outstanding or the bills paid: this balancing should be made a simple operation so a quick guide to the accuracy of the posting is obtained.

CONTROL CHECKS CAN BE CARRIED OUT

Built into all hotel billing systems should be methods of checking that all transactions are being correctly carried out and recorded. The system should be arranged so that cash sales to 'chance' guests are recorded and separated from 'charged' business. All cash should be recorded separately and the totals independently verified. A check should be made to see that all charges are being correctly posted, and finally that there is no dishonest use of the hotel's facilities by customers or staff.

IT SHOULD BE EASY TO OPERATE

The most effective hotel billing systems are those that record the individual entry the smallest number of times, and where certain procedures are carried out automatically. A complex system such as the tabular ledger will often result in a greater number of errors and omissions, to the detriment of the hotel and the discomfort of the guest. With the most modern electronic billing or computer systems the charge has only to be entered once, and it is automatically handled right up to the presentation of the bill.

IT SHOULD BE ECONOMIC IN BOTH TIME AND MONEY

The system installed must not only be economic to operate, but also economic to install. This will depend upon not only the size of the hotel, but also the tariff structure and the volume of individual transactions. A resort hotel with an inclusive daily or weekly charge can operate with a less sophisticated billing system than a 'transient' hotel of half the size. In installing a billing system a full analysis should be undertaken to establish the needs of the hotel. Part of this analysis should cover the availability of staff to operate the installed system, and the amount of management time needed to carry out control checks.

Tabular ledger

The most common method of recording charges in hotels was on the tabular ledger or 'tab'. This is an adaptation of the 'sales day book' for hotels. Although still used by smaller hotels, in many units it has been replaced by machine billing, particularly since the introduction of cheaper billing machines for small hotels. Even so the principle of the 'tab' and its double entry of charges is applicable to all forms of hotel billing.

The system revolves around two records. One is the customer's account, and the other is the tab sheet. The tab sheet is the summary of all the charges that are incurred by all guests during the day and forms the basis of the hotel's record of earnings. The customer's bill is normally prepared in duplicate, one copy being given to the guest upon departure and the other retained by the hotel for control purposes.

Layout of the tab will take one of two forms, either vertical or horizontal.

VERTICAL TABULAR LEDGER

The room numbers of guests are entered across the tab and the charges are recorded vertically below each room number. This system is often used in hotels where carbon paper is used to enter charges into both the tab and the bill at the same time. Fig. 6.1 shows the heading for a vertical tabular ledger. Each day's tab would consist of a number of similar sheets. The exact number used would depend upon the number of rooms let.

SLEEPERS 6   DATE 23 1 88

ROOM NO	101		102		104		105		103		DAILY TOTAL	
NAME	BARRETT MRS A (2)		JOSEPH MR R (1)		CONNOLLY MISS M (1)		RAY MRS S (2)		ASTLES MR A (1)			
RATE	R.O. £60		R+B £31		R.O. £30		R.O. £60		R+B £31			
B/F	62	40	12	90	14	20					89	50
APARTMENTS	60	00	29	00			60	00	29	00	178	00
PENSION												
BREAKFASTS	7	25	2	00	3	25			2	00	14	50
LUNCHEONS							14	80			14	80
TEAS				60								60
DINNERS	19	80									19	80
EARLY TEAS												
BEVERAGES						70				80	1	50
WINES	2	40									2	40
SPIRITS & LIQUEURS									4	75	4	75
BEERS			1	90							1	90
MINERALS												
TELEPHONES			4	80			12	40			17	20
V P O'S												
NEWSPAPERS												
TOTAL	151	85	51	20	18	15	87	20	36	55	344	95
CASH					18	15					18	15
ALLOWANCES	3	25									3	25
LEDGER												
BALANCE C/F	148	60	51	20			87	20	36	55	323	55

Fig. 6.1 Vertical tabular ledger

HORIZONTAL TABULAR LEDGER

The horizontal tab is more common than the vertical tab. It is easier to balance the daily total of departmental charges at the end of each day's business. The exact time of closing will depend upon the staffing of the bill office, and the pattern of work. This balancing may be carried out either at 3 p.m. or in some hotels, at 11 p.m.

With the horizontal tab, the departmental charges are listed across the tab, so each guest's account is arranged horizontally across the page of the tab. Debit charges to the guest's account are entered on the left-hand side and credit entries on the right. Normally, two lines are allowed for each room number. This enables a number of entries to be made under the departmental heading; for example a guest may have a number of telephone calls in the course of a day (*see* Fig. 6.2).

Opening bills
Few tabs are printed with the room numbers on, because occupancy generally varies too much from one period to the next. A new bill is opened by heading the bill set with the name of the guest, the number of sleepers, the rate, the room number and the date of arrival. At the same time, an entry is made in the tab showing the same information.

The tab is in room number order at the start of each day, but as departures occur and new guests arrive, this sequence is very quickly spoilt. When a new guest checks in, a tab entry must be made for them. The only place it can be made is at the end of the tab sheet. If in a 50 room hotel there are ten arrivals during a day, then these ten new arrivals will have to be entered onto the end of the sheet. The entries will be in the order that the guests arrive, not chronologically. For example, the guests for room 38 may arrive before those for room 7. For this reason, much of the time of the bill office clerks may be spent searching through the tab sheets to locate room numbers, so that they may enter charges onto the guest's account.

Posting charges
Room charges for new guests are normally entered as they arrive, and all other room charges are entered at a set time each day (for example, 6 p.m.). Other charges are entered from charge vouchers as they arrive in the bill office. The most effective method is to post the charge on to the guest's bill, and then on to the tab sheet, and finally to cross through the charge voucher

TABULAR DAILY REPORT & CONTROL OF BUSINESS DONE

DAY OF WEEK ...... TUESDAY

DATE ...... 23 JUNE

Inv. Number	Guest's Name	Room No.	Sleepers	Room	Breakfast	Food	Dinner	Bar	Wines	Telephone	Other	Daily Total	Balance B/F from Previous day	Grand Total	Cash Received	Ledger Received	Accounts Transferred to Ledger	Carried Forward
10975	GREEN MR/S	101	2	40 00	5 00		15 80	7 90	9 20			77 90	56 00	133 90				133 90
10976	BROWN MR J	102	1	25 00	2 50	4 90		2 40				34 80	35 00	69 80				69 80
10977	JAUNE MR Y	104	1	25 00	1 75					8 20		34 95	102 00	136 95		4 20		132 75
10978	PINK MS L	106	1		2 50					40		2 90	48 90	51 80	51 80			-
10979	BLACK MR/S	103	2	40 00	5 00							45 00		45 00				45 00

Fig. 6.2 Horizontal tabular ledger

to show that it has been dealt with. If a sequence such as this is always followed, then it is unlikely that any stage will be left out. Also, the bill is always up-to-date, so guests will always be charged for items they have consumed.

Allowances

If a charge is incorrectly entered, then an allowance will have to be made. This is done on the right hand side of the tab, and on the credit section of the bill.

For example, a breakfast charge of £3 may be incorrectly charged to room 38 instead of room 83. The guest in room 38 will have a credit entry made on their bill and a corresponding entry on the tab and in the allowance book. Then the charge will be correctly entered on to the account of room 83. An entry will also be made in the allowance book, which is checked daily by management. This explains the reason for each allowance, and acts as a quick control check.

Departures

As a guest checks out their bill is totalled and the top copy presented to them for payment. The method of payment is noted on the bill and the carbon copy, and the bill is receipted. The tab is then totalled to agree with the bill, and the payment entered in the appropriate column on the credit side of the tab. A pencil line is then drawn through the guest's name and room number. This serves two purposes. Firstly, it shows that the guest has checked out, and secondly, it ensures that no charges for an incoming guest are inadvertently posted into the wrong account.

Room changes

If a guest changes room during their stay, then the new number has to be noted on both the bill and the tab. This is done by crossing the old room number through and writing the new room number above it. When this happens the bill office clerk has to make sure that checks from departments are posted to the correct room number.

Cash sales

Cash sales from the restaurant and bars will be recorded on the tab ledger, along with the rest of the day's business. In this way the tab is a complete record of the hotel's trading for a 24 hour period.

Balancing

The basis of all double-entry book-keeping is the ability to 'balance' at the end of the day's trading. The balance ensures that both sides of the account are equal.

The major balancing features are:

1 the debit side will equal the credit side;
2 cash taken should equal the cash column of the tab;
3 the credit column should equal transfers to ledger;
4 the carried forward column will be equal to the total of outstanding bills.

Further balances may be carried out between each column and the individual checks. Even though these balancing checks are carried out there are some errors which will not be located during balances. A bill voucher may not be posted to a guest's account at all. This may not be notified until the guest has departed (error of omission). A voucher may be either posted to the wrong account or the wrong amount may be posted. Again, this may not be noticed for some time (error of commission). Finally, a compensating error may be made. This usually takes the form of a wrong addition on two sides of the tab which allows the tab to balance even though the accounts are wrong (compensating error). Fig. 6.2 shows a horizontal tab with some entries made. Although only nine debit columns are shown in the example tabular ledger (*see* Fig. 6.2) it is common for there to be as many as the hotel requires. Often there will be fifteen or more on the debit side of the tab. This will reflect the amount of analysis the hotel wishes to carry out.

To balance: addition of Columns 1–9 = Column 10.

Column 10 and 11 = Column 12 total
Column 12 = Column 13 + 14 + 15 + 16.

Figure 6.3 shows the bill of an individual guest (room 106) with the same entries as on the tabular ledger.

Many hotels that operate a tab ledger produce two guest bills. One is a three-day bill for short stay guests, and the other is an eight-day bill for guests who stay for a longer time. The bills are exactly the same, apart from the greater number of columns on the eight-day bill.

ROOM No. 106

INVOICE No. 10978

DUKES' HOTEL

Great Pulteney Street,
Bath, Avon.
BA2 4DN
Telephone (0225) 63512

Miss L. Pink

VAT No. 398 7405 95

Peter F. Yarker, F.H.C.I.M.A., Master Innholder, M.Inst.M.

Date	23/6							
Accommodation & Breakfast	2	50						
Dinner								
Teas/Coffees								
Other Foods								
Bar Drinks								
Wines								
Newspapers								
Telephone		40						
Daily Total	2	90						
Brought Forward	48	90						
Carried Forward	51	80						

Fig. 6.3 Manual guest bill

Machine billing

Using machines for hotel billing is essentially the same as the tabular ledger. All that the machine does is to carry out some of the tasks of the bill office automatically, as charges are being posted. The principle of double-entry book-keeping is exactly the same.

A hotel billing machine should be thought of as two machines in one. The first acts as an adding machine and posts charges onto guests' bills and notes the new balance. The second keeps a cumulative total of the amount charged to each department.

There are two distinct forms of machine now in use in hotels. The original type, electromechanical, make use of electric power to drive cogs and gears which carry out posting and balancing. This form of machine has been in existence for many years, and includes NCR 42 and Sweda 1000. They are still in use in many hotels, but are no longer manufactured and so as they fall into disrepair they are replaced, either by computers, or by the second type of machine, the electronic.

An electronic machine uses printed circuits to carry out the work of the bill office, and the only mechanical section is the printer for the bill, and the audit roll.

Electronic machines can be simple, and merely duplicate the work of an electromechanical register; the more sophisticated ones will be able to carry out more complex tasks such as analysis of individual item sales, and automatic balancing. As there are fewer moving parts in electronic machines, they are less likely to break down, are quieter in operation, and also require less maintenance.

BENEFITS OF MACHINE BILLING

Machine accounting has the following advantages over the tabular ledger:

1 Simultaneous posting. Both entries are made at the same time so agreement between the bill and ledger is assured;
2 Mechanical addition. The machine does the addition (or subtraction) and so no errors will be made;
3 Legible presentation. The bill is mechanically prepared so all figures will be clear and uniform. Even a neat bill written in two different hands can look untidy;
4 Automatic verification of charge vouchers. Many of the machines in existence allow the charge voucher to be cancelled at the same time as it is posted. This cuts down control work;
5 Bills on demand. As the new balance is automatically printed

each time a charge is posted the bill is ready at any time of the day or night;

6 Built-in control. All machines have a number of easy control checks which can quickly ensure that all charges and income are correctly recorded by the bill office clerk. The audit roll provides a complete record of every transaction on the machine, so an exhaustive check of each shift is possible.

OPERATING A BILLING MACHINE

The keyboard of a machine has a number of groups of keys:

1 Figure keys. These are the keys that are used to post the amounts of charges, and room numbers;

2 Storage keys. There are two types of storage key; debit and credit. They correspond exactly to the analysis columns on the tab. These keys automatically keep a running total of every entry onto them;

3 Sub-analysis keys. Storage keys can be further analysed by using sub-analysis keys. These keys may be used to show whether a particular meal was breakfast (B), lunch (L) or dinner (D). The information is posted onto the bill and also the audit roll.

4 Addition keys. Pick up, sub-total and total keys merely carry out additions and subtractions. They do not store any totals;

5 Operator keys. Some machines have separate keys for each clerk. In this way it is possible to identify the entries of individual clerks on one shift;

6 X and Z keys. These are the keys which allow the trial balance or balance to be carried out at the end of each shift. The Z key is normally held by management and not only reads the total, but clears the machine for the next shift.

OPENING A BILL

The bill is headed with the guest's name, tariff and room number. In some hotels, it is normal to post a zero balance onto the bill to show that it is a new account, rather than a continuation bill.

POSTING OF CHARGES

The room number is entered and if the bill has a previous balance this must be entered. Electronic machines will not allow an incorrect balance to be picked up. The amount of the charge is entered on the figure keys and the appropriate analysis key is pressed. Many machines now have pre-set rates and so the charge is made automatically. Many machines carry a 'proving' slot, the voucher is placed here and the transaction will be printed on the voucher, proving that the bill clerk has entered the charge. The new balance key should be pressed at the end of the transaction, providing the bill with a new total. The bill should then be returned to the tray in room number order.

With one sequence the following tasks have been carried out:

1 the charge posted to the bill;
2 the new balance calculated;
3 the charge voucher has been overprinted to prove the posting;
4 the amount has been allocated to the appropriate department;
5 a record has been made on the audit roll for subsequent control checks.

ADJUSTMENTS/CORRECTIONS

If a voucher has been overcharged, or charged to the wrong account or department then it will be necessary to correct the error. Most machines carry an allowance or adjustment key enabling the amount of the error to be credited to the guest's bill. Many hotels also keep a book, or daily sheet where these corrections are noted and an explanation added.

CLOSING AN ACCOUNT

Some machines have a 'paid in full' key which automatically receipts the bill at the end of the guest's stay. Whether the bill is paid cash or transferred to ledger the initial procedure is the same. Ensure that all charges have been added to the account and, where appropriate, the telephone meter has been read.

The bill should be presented to the client and the method of payment ascertained. Cash payments should be keyed into the paid in full/cash key which will subsequently reduce the balance on the bill to zero, showing that the account is closed. Ledger payments will be transferred to the ledger paid key, either at once, or summarised and transferred at the end of the shift. The top copy of the bill is given to the guest and the bottom copy is kept by the hotel (*see* Fig. 6.4)

BALANCING THE MACHINE

At the end of the shift the machine will be balanced before handing over to the next shift. This is done using the X key. After a day's trading the machine will be cleared completely. To clear the machine the Z key is used. This key is normally held by a senior member of staff to ensure that the machine is only cleared when it is authorised. A Z reading may be taken at any time in

		Room No.
		221

EROS HOTEL

69 SHAFTESBURY AVENUE LONDON W1V 8EX
Telephone: 01-734 8781 Telex: 268564 EROSHT

Rate	£ 63.50
Number of Guests	2

A/c to.......... OWN A/C ....

Address. ....

....

....

Arrival Date	18/6
No. Nights	1
Departure Date	19/6

Guest's Name:...... Mr/s W. Wilson ....

Deposit Received					
Voucher No.		Date	Ref. No.	Code	Amount

**All prices are FULLY INCLUSIVE
(VAT at   %)**

INVOICE: 65552

```
                    19/06/86#1070
                    PLAN#2**********63.50
                                            WILSON
                    DBAL                      .00
                      23        2.00
                    FOOD        4.00
                    PAPERS       .50
                    BAL  A1    1# 221-2***    4.50

                    19/06/86#1071
                    DBAL                     4.50
                    PLAN#2     63.50
                      203        .14
                    PHONE       2.80
                    GARAGE      3.50
                    BAR  #2     5.00
                    BAL  A1    1# 221-2***   79.30
```

VAT Registration No. 340 1934 84		
Hotel Services		
VAT at %		
Sub-Total		
Paid outs		
TOTAL		

```
                    19/06/86#1072
                    DBAL                    79.30
                    TOTL                    79.30
                    CASH              79.30
                    BAL  A1    1# 221  ***    .00
                    NET        68.52
                    VAT        10.28
                    -15.000%
```

PLEASE LEAVE YOUR KEY

**PLEASE OBTAIN AN OFFICIAL RECEIPT
FOR ALL PAYMENTS**

Fig. 6.4 Electronic billing machine

95

the 24 hour period, dependent upon the operation. Smaller units may close the books around 3 p.m. whilst large hotels may employ night auditors who will balance the machine and prepare management reports between 11 p.m. and 8 a.m.

The balance is always calculated and agreed using the X key, and when both sides balance, the Z key is used to clear the machine. This means that all departmental totals can be verified before they are cleared.

The procedure of balancing is exactly the same as that of balancing the tab. The debit side must equal the total credits.

With the machine the balance is carried out in the following way:

(a) X key is placed in machine;
(b) summary card placed on tray;
(c) X reading of debit keys;
(d) sub-total;
(e) add on brought forward (previous day's balance);
(f) sub-total;
(g) X reading of credit keys;
(h) new balance;
(i) add list current bills.

If the machine total (h) equals the total of all the current bills in the tray (i) then the machine balances and a Z reading can be taken. It is rare that the machine will balance correctly first time, and then a search has to be made for mistakes.

Fault finding in accounting machines is a skilled task, and many clerks seem to know intuitively where to look for mistakes.

In searching for errors it is essential to follow a systematic pattern. This pattern should look first of all at the easiest tasks to check, and then proceed to the more difficult and time-consuming tasks. Simple faults that are easy to check are: that the brought forward total is correct; that no bills are missing from the bill tray; and that all the bills have been totalled correctly.

Balancing an electronic machine is far simpler than balancing an electromechanical because many of the traditional errors have been eliminated. A very common error is the picking up of an incorrect balance and electronic machines will not accept a bill if an error of this type has been made.

PREPARING FOR THE NEXT SHIFT

The final tasks after balancing the machine are to enter the depart-mental totals onto a summary sheet, change the audit roll and change the date wheel on the machine. Many electronic machines will automatically change the date as the 'Z' reading is made. When the machine has been cleared and the audit roll changed the bill office clerk usually takes an 'X' reading. This shows the next shift that the machine was clear. If the hotel make the balance at 3 p.m. obviously the date will not be changed at the same time— that becomes the responsibility of the shift leader in the evening.

Computer billing

Many people erroneously believe that only large hotels will benefit from the use of a computer, but billing this way can be cost effective even for the smallest hotel. Many systems can be linked to other areas such as the switchboard and for some hotels the computer system has expanded to ensure that staff no longer waste time doing boring work but have more time to spend looking after the guests.

BENEFITS OF COMPUTER BILLING

All the benefits of machine billing are equally applicable to a computer, but additionally a computer will eliminate even more of the tedious work which is associated with the making up of accounts.

OPERATING A COMPUTER

The operation of the computer will vary according to the system—unlike electronic machines they follow no pattern— nevertheless it is possible to make one or two generalisations:

1 Room charges will be processed automatically;
2 VAT will be calculated at the appropriate rate excluding items which are zero rated;
3 A wrong charge will not be accepted onto a bill if the error is user induced.

OPENING A BILL

If the reservation is an advanced booking guest details will already be stored, but the room number can be added effortlessly and the information amended if necessary. Advance deposits which have already been recorded will be transferred to the account after check in.

POSTING CHARGES

If the system includes terminals at point of sales a great deal of time is saved posting charges. The information can be entered directly in the sales area and the bill office clerk is saved the monotony of sorting and posting vouchers. Many of the charges (e.g. wine, sauna, apartments) are pre-coded, but the codes used to analyse the transactions are easily identifiable (*see* Fig. 6.5).

```
                               Royal Garden Hotel
                 Kensington High Street, London W8 4PT  01-937 8000 Telex 263151 Cables ROYGARTEL London W8
            MR. EDWARD FLETCHER                         ROOM      51003
            MRS. EDWARD FLETCHER                        NG
                                                        CREDIT CARD
                                                        ARRIVAL DATE     04/05/87 @ 21:59
            UNITED STATES OF AMERICA                    DEPARTURE DATE   07/05/87
            07/05/87  17:29                             AX378262674401005

   DATE     TIME     DESCRIPTION                         VAT %    DEBIT    CREDIT

   04 MAY   22.49    GARDEN CAFE DINNER 0282             15.0     27.60
            23.37    GARDEN BAR 0302                     15.0     12.60
            23.37    GARDEN BAR GRATUITIES 0302          EXMPT     3.00
            00.00    APARTMENTS (AUTO)                   15.0    144.00
            00.21    FLOOR SERVICE 0305                  15.0     14.40
            00.21    FLOOR SERVICE GRATUITIES 0305       EXMPT     2.00
            00.00    TELEPHONE (AUTO)                    15.0      0.55
   05 MAY   09.15    ROYAL ROOF GRATUITIES 0061          EXMPT     4.00
            09.15    ROYAL ROOF BREAKFAST 0061           15.0     22.00
            21.40    GARDEN CAFE DINNER 0314             15.0     30.60
            21.40    GARDEN CAFE GRATUITIES 0314         EXMPT     4.00
            22.32    GARDEN BAR 0379                     15.0     12.30
            22.32    GARDEN BAR GRATUITIES 0379          EXMPT     1.00
            00.16    APARTMENTS (AUTO)                   15.0    144.00
   06 MAY   09.00    GARDEN CAFE BREAKFAST 0117          15.0     17.00
            23.29    GARDEN BAR 0457                     15.0      4.50
            23.29    GARDEN BAR GRATUITIES 0457          EXMPT     1.00
            00.22    APARTMENTS (AUTO)                   15.0    144.00
            00.00    TELEPHONE (AUTO)                    15.0      1.80
   07 MAY   07.30    GARDEN CAFE BREAKFAST 0078          15.0     13.00
                     TRANSFERRED FROM 1003
   07 MAY   17:29    BALANCE DUE                         *****   603.35
                     AMOUNT TO BE SETTLED BY GUEST £603.35
```

Royal Garden Hotel (Oddenino's) Limited, Kensington High Street, London W8 4PT
Registered in England No 827986, Registered Office 6 Connaught Place, London W2 2EZ
A Company within The Rank Organisation
Value Added Tax Registration Number 239 4563 39

Rank Hotels

Fig. 6.5 Computerised bill

ADJUSTMENTS/CORRECTIONS

Entries to alter previous postings can be made easily, and should it be necessary to move a guest to another room all the existing data will be transferred to the new room.

CLOSING AN ACCOUNT

Once the guest has agreed the total the computer can be advised how payment is to be made—either in cash or transferred to an account. If the guest has previously indicated that all, or part, of the bill is to be transferred elsewhere this can be carried out automatically and quickly. In some systems the computer will be programmed only to accept certain charges on main accounts, all else being transferred to extras bills.

BALANCING

Balancing as such does not really exist with a computer, since so many possible errors have been eliminated at source.

Information is readily available and the audit trail can be displayed at any time. The end of the day routine is quick and easy, and in some establishments is little more than an automatic accounting record for the day's business. There is, however, a selection of reports and information (i.e. rooms' sales, projected sleeper occupancy) readily available to management providing them with the vital up-to-the-minute information essential for effective forward planning.

Control procedures

The basis of control is the independent checking of accounts and charges in the hotel. This is important in any business, but particularly so where cash, food and drink are concerned.

The level of control has to be balanced against the cost of finding and rectifying errors. At a certain stage it is cheaper to allow errors to go undetected because the cost of locating them would be prohibitive. Some hotels overcome this by randomly changing the area of strict control so that a close check is made in each area at some stage. Many hotels no longer operate a control office as such, preferring instead to rely upon the increased efficiency of the machinery in use throughout the establishment.

Regardless of the system in operation a simple check is normally performed to control the apartment income revenue. Room charges are controlled by agreeing three separate figures; any discrepancies must be followed through and checked. Fig. 6.6

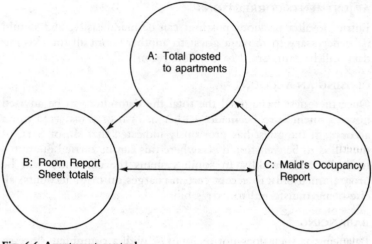

Fig. 6.6 Apartment control

shows the apartment control triangle. A, B and C should be prepared independently of each other and A = B = C.

In some establishments a further check may be made on linen used to ensure that all the rooms have been correctly reported.

Night audit

Large hotels make use of night auditors who work between 11 p.m. and 8 a.m. to carry out control tasks, post charges, prepare management reports, and balance the hotel's daily trading accounts. In some units the night auditor will also carry out the separate tasks of night manager, receptionist and security officer.

If the hotel has a late night food and beverage service, and a busy desk, then a night auditor will be very useful for he or she will be able to carry out posting though the night. In this way guest accounts will be fully up-to-date in time for morning departures. A night auditor brings forward by eight hours control procedures and checks on posting and balancing. These eight hours may be critical, for an error may be located and re-posted onto a guest's account before departure. Often if a guest leaves before an account is corrected the charge has to be written off as a bad debt.

Potential bad debts

The different pace of work at night and the absence of interruption allows the night auditor to check through current
accounts in the bill tray in order to identify guests who may be
potential bad debts. The first method is to list all bills over a
certain figure for the attention of the head cashier. The head
cashier is then able to check the booking details to establish the
status of the guest. Certainly a chance guest would be a greater
credit risk than a guest with a confirmed booking. A second
method of identifying potential 'walk-outs' is to check the individual bills for unusual spending patterns. A guest who orders
large amounts of liquor from floor service, or who has high food
and beverage charges, may be ordering them in the expectation
of not paying the bill at the end of their stay.

In the case of a guest who was thought to be a potential 'walk-
out' or 'bad debt', the hotel security officer or assistant manager
would check up on:

1 details of booking;
2 registration card and information;
3 contents of room and luggage;
4 any telephone calls placed through the operator.

All of these checks are carried out discreetly, often without the
guest knowing they are going on. The check on luggage would
be done when the guest was out of the hotel. If the checks were
not satisfactory, then the room would be double locked and the
guest contacted and asked to bring their bill up-to-date. Obviously,
care needs to be taken in this aspect of control work and consequently it is normally assigned to a senior and experienced
member of staff.

Self assessment questions

1 List four objectives of a hotel billing system.
2 Explain how a charge is posted onto a tabular ledger.
3 What are the benefits of machine accounting.
4 What are the benefits of computer billing.
5 Show how apartment income is controlled.
6 What are the major advantages of a night audit department in a large hotel.

Chapter 7

CASHIER AND METHODS OF PAYMENT

Chapter objectives

After studying this chapter you should be able to:
- identify the characteristics of the various methods of payment;
- compare systems of handling safe deposit of guests' property;
- show how income is banked and how elementary control procedures are established.

Cash floats

Every hotel will need a store or 'float' of money to enable it to provide service to the customers, to give charge for bills, to allow the bars and other sales points to operate, and to carry out foreign exchange transactions (within policy limits).

SIZE OF FLOATS

The number of floats in a hotel will vary according to the number of sales outlets; a very small hotel may have just one float, whilst a large hotel with many restaurants may have ten or more separate floats, one for each sales point. The amount of money needed in the float will be a reflection of two things. Firstly the prices charged in the departments, and secondly, the number of transactions that are carried out. The higher the number of separate transactions, the greater the size of the float. Another factor that has to be considered is the method of payment used. A hotel that has a large number of foreign guests will need a larger float, for it will not be able to use their foreign currency payments to give change to later customers.

COMPOSITION OF FLOATS

Individual floats are made up to the agreed amount in a predetermined way. This composition will again reflect the tariffs of the department concerned. The main cash float of a large hotel will not have a great need for low value coins, for most items will come to round figures. However, this will not be the case in a bar or kiosk. The float is stored in a secure cash drawer in the same way in every department; this enables cashiers to relieve each other, or transfer from one department to another with the minimum of interference to the process of giving change rapidly and accurately. The layout of the coins in the cash drawer is organised so that a contrast is made between the coins which lie next to each other. For example, 50p pieces will be placed next to 5p pieces so that the cashier will not confuse the two by texture, size or weight.

SECURITY

Cash floats are signed for as they are issued, and signed back in again at the end of the day. If there is a handover from one shift to another, then the total amount in the cash drawer is counted and agreed, and the float is passed over to the incoming cashier. Floats are occasionally subjected to spot checks by auditors to ensure that they are correct and that no irregularities are occurring. Particularly dangerous would be personal IOUs in floats from individual cashiers. This is forbidden as it reduces the actual cash available to the business and aids the cashier in certain frauds and thefts.

COST OF MONEY

The aim of the hotel should be to keep the number of floats and the amount of money in them to the lowest level possible, while still allowing the business to run smoothly. The first reason for this is the risk of theft or robbery. A large amount of money will be more attractive to a thief. In the event of a robbery, the loss will be minimised.

A float also costs money to provide. Any money that the hotel has that is not in the bank is not earning interest or reducing the size of the overdraft. For example, if the interest rate is 15 per cent per annum then a £1000 float will cost £150 per year to maintain in the hotel. If the float can be safely reduced to £500, then the hotel is able to add £75 to its profit at the end of the year.

Methods of payment

Upon departure, guests can settle their account in one of nine different ways. These are:

1 cash;
2 foreign currency;

3 cheque;
4 travellers cheque;
5 eurocheque
6 credit card
7 charge card
8 ledger payment
9 voucher (e.g. travel agent, A & TO)

In dealing with each of these methods of payment, the hotelier must assess the impact of three major factors:

1 liquidity;
2 security;
3 worth.

Liquidity
If a bill is paid in cash the hotel can immediately use the money to purchase goods itself, or bank the money and earn interest on it. Payment by ledger, however, will take much longer—perhaps as much as two or three months may pass before the money can be re-used in the business. The relative liquidity of the payment methods is shown in Fig. 7.1).

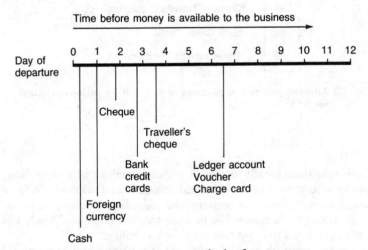

Fig. 7.1 Relative liquidity of various methods of payment

Security
There are two sides to security. The first is the likelihood of forgery or fraud by each of the payment methods; the second is the subsequent risk of theft once the hotel has the money.

Payment by cheque is a greater security risk than accepting dollars in payment of the account. But if the hotel was robbed, it would be very difficult to trace stolen currency, whereas cheques would be unlikely to be taken as they would be worthless to a thief.

Worth

Finally, there is the total amount of money the hotel eventually receives in payment. This will not be the same in every case.

Handling charges, commission and delays in payment all cost the hotel money. On the other hand, because of the extra commission, accepting payment in foreign currency often means that the hotel gains an extra profit when guests use this method of payment. Fig. 7.2 shows the amounts received in payment of a bill for £100. Reference to this index clearly shows that the profitability of the hotel may be affected by the variety of payment methods used by its guests.

102	Foreign Currency
100	Sterling
98	Cheques/Travellers' cheques/Ledger
96	Bank Credit Cards
89	Travel Agent's Vouchers

Fig. 7.2 Amount received in payment of £100 bill by various payment methods

CASH

Cash was traditionally the most popular method of paying bills, but as prices have risen it is used less in hotels where bills for a few days stay can often amount to hundreds of pounds. Payment in Scottish pound notes may be accepted, but Channel Islands and Irish currency can only be exchanged at banks.

Theoretically, there are upper limits for payment in coin as legal tender. These are:

1 bronze (2p, 1p)—20p total;
2 cupro-nickel (20p, 10p, 5p)—£5 total;
3 50p pieces—£10 total;
4 £1 coins—no limit theoretically.

A hotel may insist on payment in legal tender (cash). Nevertheless all other methods of payment are accepted as a service to customers. Any hotel that insisted upon cash only as a method of settling bills would probably lose a lot of business as a result.

FOREIGN CURRENCY

Tourists and overseas visitors often wish to settle their bill in their own currency. A list of currencies accepted and the exchange rate is kept in the cashiers department. The currencies of the eastern European block and other countries that are subject to severe exchange rate fluctuation are not accepted. The rate of exchange that the hotel offers is generally less favourable than could be obtained at a bank. This commission covers the cost of providing the service, guards against a sudden change in the exchange rate, and provides the hotel with an extra profit. Coins are not accepted in hotels although some major banks will accept them at around 80 per cent of the current note exchange rate.

In recent years, foreign exchange has become more complex through the 'floating' of sterling against other currencies. This means that the exchange rate will vary over a year, and even from one day to the next. Group hotels overcome this by notifying individual units of the exact rate to offer. Smaller units can either check with their bank or look in the current daily paper where major exchange rates are listed. It is a simple matter to add on a fixed percentage to this rate to cover the hotel's costs.

Cashiers have to be trained in the recognition of the major currencies in order to avoid the risk of crude forgeries being passed off as genuine. This also ensures that the cashier will recognise different currencies with the same name such as American and Canadian dollars.

CHEQUES

The growth of cheques has reflected the decline of cash as a method of payment in recent years. This has been aided by the introduction of cheque guarantee cards (*see* Fig. 7.3). These cards guarantee payment of the cheque up to an agreed amount (currently £50) provided that a few simple rules are followed:

1 only one cheque is used per transaction;
2 it is signed in the presence of the cashier;
3 the bank code on the cheque and the guarantee card agree (not visa);
4 the card number is written on the reverse side of the cheque;
5 the card has not expired.

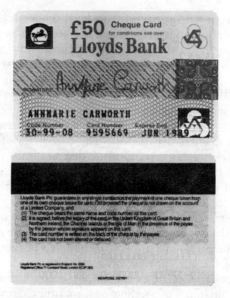

Fig. 7.3 Cheque guarantee card

It is not possible to pay a bill of £100 and issue two cheques of £50, for the bank does not guarantee to honour this transaction. By putting the card number on the back of the cheque, the transaction is changed to a cash one, and the customer will not be able to stop the cheque later. It is important that the cashier watches the customer sign the cheque and then compares the signatures carefully to establish that they are similar.

Code number
The bank sorting code number must agree with the code of the issuing cheque.

Card number
The card number is written on the reverse of the cheque by the accepting cashier. It does not correspond to any other number on the cheque.

Expiry date
The card will not be valid if it is out of date.

Signature
The signature must be checked against the signature written on

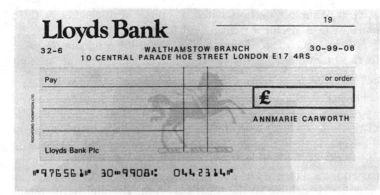

Fig. 7.4 Cheque

the cheque. The card should be examined to make sure that the signature panel has not been tampered with.

Figure 7.4 shows a typical cheque. Most cheques are now issued crossed and so have to be paid into a bank account. They can be reassigned to a third party by the payee signing on the back. But if a third party cheque is returned, then the hotel has to contact the original drawer of the cheque to obtain settlement. For this reason, hotels do not usually accept third party cheques.

When accepting a cheque, the cashier should ensure:

1 That the date is correct; a cheque which has a date in the future on it (postdated) will not become valid until that date. A cheque more than six months old ('stale') is no longer valid;
2 That the words and figures agree. If they do not, the cheque will not be paid at all;
3 That it is correctly signed, preferably in sight of the cashier;
4 That it is completed in ink rather than in pencil;
5 That any alterations are signed (not initialled) by the drawer.

Blank cheques used to be held by some hotels so that a customer could fill in the details of their own bank and account number while paying the bill. As the risk of fraud is much greater with cheques of this kind, the banks discourage their use by levying a high service charge on cheques that are paid in by this method. Payment will also take longer as the cheque cannot be electronically sorted.

There are a number of conventions about crossing cheques. The two most important are:

1 A/c payee. This allows the cheque only to be paid into the

account of the person nominated. It cannot be assigned to a third party. This is useful for cheques that are sent by post;
2 Not to exceed £xx. This crossing establishes a maximum value to the cheque to guard against fraud by changing the amount payable.

During banking hours a hotel cashier can quickly establish whether a cheque is good for payment. A telephone call is made to the hotel's bank, with details of the cheque, and the name of the bank and the branch. The bank will contact the manager of the drawer's branch and establish whether the cheque will be passed for payment. The cost of the telephone call for this 'special clearance' is debited to the hotel's account, although some establishments pass it onto the guest. A 'special clearance' is useful when checking out a chance guest whose bill is greater than the cheque card limit (*see* Fig. 7.5).

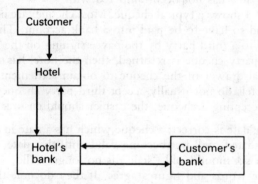

Fig. 7.5 Special clearance for a cheque during banking hours

TRAVELLERS CHEQUES

These are issued in fixed denominations by major banks and travel agents throughout the world. The customer buys them (before leaving home) in their own currency, or in the currency of the country being visited. When they are purchased they have to be signed, and the serial numbers are noted by the issuing bank cashier. Normally a service charge of 1 per cent is paid to the bank by the customer. This covers insurance against loss or theft. If the travellers cheques are stolen the issuing company will repay the customer within 24 hours. For this reason travellers cheques are much more secure than currency. When accepting payment by travellers cheque the cashier should watch the guest sign and date the cheque. If there is any doubt about the signature the customer

Fig. 7.6 Traveller's cheque
   (1) Sterling
   (2) Dollars

can be asked to sign·again on the reverse of the cheque. This is a very potent weapon against fraud as few people are able to forge a signature without one to copy. Proof of identity can also be verified by asking the guest to produce their passport before accepting the travellers cheque.

Travellers cheques must then be paid into the bank account of the hotel, normally with the room number of the guest noted on the reverse side so that any queries that arise later can be followed up (*see* Fig. 7.6).

EUROCHEQUES

As the name implies these are cheques which are mainly used while travellers are abroad. Many tourists and overseas visitors wish to settle their account in their own currency and may not wish to carry cash. Eurocheques differ from ordinary travellers cheques in that they are drawn, just like a cheque, on the drawers'

Lloyds Bank 30-99-08

Walthamstow Branch
10 Central Parade Hoe Street London E17 4RS

UK

Pay against this cheque the sum of
Payez contre ce chèque / Zahlen Sie gegen diesen Scheck

Currency
Dev./Währg | Amount / Montant / Betrag

Amount in words / Somme en toutes lettres / Betrag in Buchstaben

To / à / an

Place / Lieu / Ort

Date / Datum

Signature / Unterschrift

ANNMARIE CARWORTH

LLOYDS BANK PLC   Account No

⑈424321⑈ 30⑈9908⑆ 0442314⑈ 08

No writing or stamping in this space / Laisser cette partie en blanc / Dieses Feld nicht beschriften und nicht bestempeln

Fig. 7.7 Eurocheque

own account. They are usually written in the local currency and
include some of the information which appears on an ordinary
cheque (*see* Fig. 7.7).

They are supported by a eurocheque card, up to a maximum
guaranteed sum, which varies from one country to another (*see*
Fig. 7.8).

Fig. 7.8 Eurocheque card

Like an ordinary cheque there are certain points which must be observed before payment is guaranteed:

1 It must be signed in the presence of the paying cashier;
2 The signature on the cheque and the card must agree;
3 The name of the bank and its code number must be the same on the card and the cheque;
4 The card number must be written on the reverse of the cheque by the accepting cashier;
5 The card must be within the date limit (i.e. not expired).

In the UK the maximum amount guaranteed is currently £100, and this standardised system of cheques for overseas travel is obviously very helpful to the hotel, eliminating the risk traditionally associated with cheques drawn on overseas banks, yet still providing a service for the client.

BANK CREDIT CARDS

The two major bank credit cards in the UK are Visa and Access. The cards are issued free to customers and there is no annual subscription. The customer uses the card to purchase goods and services by signing a sales voucher for the total amount of the bill. At monthly intervals the card company sends a statement to the customer detailing all purchases in the previous month. The customer may pay the total owing, or pay only a portion of it and pay the rest over a period of time. The minimum payment is fixed by the government as the cards constitute a form of credit.

In June 1987 the minimum repayment was 5 per cent or £5 whichever is the greater. So a bill of £100 would require a payment of £5, but a bill of £10 would still need a payment of £5. The service charge is 1.75 per cent per month or 23.1 per cent per year. This is the interest charge on the money that the user has in effect borrowed from the bank. This varies from time to

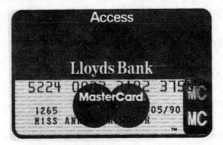

Fig. 7.9 Access card (Mastercard and Eurocard)

time with market interest rates. When the card is obtained the customer receives a personal credit limit, and that must not be exceeded in any one month.

Visa is an internationally recognised name, and while most countries use an additional name (e.g. UK—Barclaycard, France—Carte Bleue) all cards carry the name VISA and bear the distinctive blue, white and gold stripe.

Access is also international, with world-wide circulation, but it is affiliated to two major cards in other countries and so can also be used at establishments displaying signs for Mastercharge or Eurocard. Access cards issued in the UK will bear the logo of all three companies (*see* Fig. 7.9).

ELECTRONIC TRANSFER AT POINT OF SALE

Initially launched in France this is now a fast growing method of payment in the UK. A microchip embedded in the plastic of the card records the details of the transaction when the card is used in conjunction with the computer terminal at the point of sale.

Barclays CONNECT card allows goods or services to be signed for and is debited to a client's current account at once.

CHARGE CARDS

Charge cards, sometimes called T and E cards, are different in a number of ways. The customer has to pay an annual subscription for the card and has to settle each month's statement in full; there are no facilities for extending repayment. Generally, the credit limit on T and E cards will be higher, and they are more likely to be used for the purchase of airline tickets, hotel bills and restaurant bills. The procedure for accepting payment by each type of card is broadly the same. The card company issues a franchise to the hotel which enables it to accept the cards in payment. The hotel is given a 'floor limit' which sets the maximum amount that can be paid by the card without telephoning for authorisation. All major card companies operate a 24 hour authorisation centre where a cashier may make a reverse charge call to check on the validity of a card or obtain clearance to accept payment of a bill above the floor limit. Many front office computer systems also keep a 'stop list' of lost or stolen cards.

Procedure for payment by credit card
1 Check that bill is inside 'floor limit';
2 prepare sales voucher;

3 obtain card from client;
4 take imprint of card on sales voucher;
5 pass voucher to client to sign (retain card);
6 check that signatures on card and voucher agree;
7 return card and top copy of voucher to guest.

At this point the procedure for dealing with the two card types differs. Charge card sales vouchers are sent to the card company every few weeks, and a cheque is returned in payment with the commission to the card company substracted. Bank card sales vouchers are paid into the bank along with cash and cheques, and are debited to the hotel's account in the normal way, again minus a commission charge. The rate of commission will be different between the different card companies, but is commonly between 2–5 per cent of the amount billed. The franchise issued by the card companies prohibits the hotel from adding the commission as a surcharge onto the bill of the guest. Because of the different operating systems, bills paid by charge cards take longer to settle than bills which are paid by bank credit cards.

LEDGER ACCOUNTS

To encourage customer loyalty, and for convenience, many hotels allow their guests to sign the bill as they depart, and arrange for all charges to be sent to the company or the individual at the end of the month for settlement. Ledger payment facilities are only offered after the hotel has established that the customer is creditworthy, either by obtaining satisfactory references from another supplier, or from the customer's bank. Obviously with a deferred payment there is a greater risk of bad debt, and certainly the hotel will have to wait to get its money, sometimes as much as two or three months after the bill was incurred. When opening a ledger account for a company the hotel has to obtain a list of authorised users, and agree a limit for individual bills. Some ledger accounts are partial only, the guest being allowed to charge the company for accommodation and meals, but responsible for extras such as laundry and telephone calls. In this case the bill office must run two bills for the guest. Many large hotels or chains operate their own in-house credit card scheme, such as Inncard or Trustcard, and this is obviously preferable to the hotel, since they need pay no comission. Many hotels feel that the existence of ledger accounts encourages the users to choose their hotel more frequently, and to spend a greater amount of money.

VOUCHERS

Travel agents issue vouchers to customers to enable them to settle their hotel bills. This is simply an extension of the ledger system, and the hotel has to take similar precautions to ensure that the agent is reputable. The voucher is normally for specified services and one copy is sent to the hotel with the booking, and the top copy obtained from the client on arrival. All the vouchers from a particular agent are returned, usually at the end of the month, for payment and when the agent pays the bill they will usually subtract their commission on the accommodation and breakfast charges.

Vouchers can often cause problems for cashiers, since they may be issued in a foreign currency and the exchange rate may have changed. In addition some overseas agents may be using out-of-date tariffs, or the voucher may even be the confirmation of a booking, rather than of actual monetary worth. Thomas Cook intend to overcome most of these of problems by the phasing in of their **International Service Order**, which confirms bookings and guarantees prompt payment of the service provided by the hotel.

When a booking is made in a hotel an International Service Order will be issued which guarantees payment for the specified value—as with a voucher there will be one copy for the customer and one copy for the hotel. The client will surrender their copy in exchange for the service provided by the hotel, and will pay direct for any additional charges. To obtain payment for the value shown on the International Service Order the hotel merely sends their invoice together with the copy of the client's voucher to Thomas Cook. Providing the details on the invoice correspond with those on the International Service Order the computer based system will automatically raise a cheque which will be despatched within seven days.

The advantages of this system are clear in that the service orders will be reduced to one simple document, easily recognised and easy to process (*see* Fig. 7.10).

Foreign exchange

Large hotels with a high proportion of overseas visitors will make a contribution to their annual profit by offering foreign exchange facilities to their guests. The service is offered on a one way basis only. The hotel may sell sterling for a foreign currency. If a guest wishes to buy foreign currency then they have to use a bank.

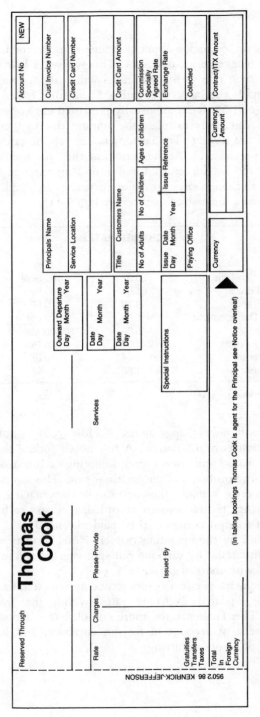

Fig. 7.10 International service order

There is no legislation about exchange rates, so the hotel is free to offer whatever price it wishes. This is always lower than the bank exchange rate so that the hotel will make a profit on each transaction. If the bank is charging $1.52 for £1 then the hotel may charge $1.55. Rates are usually presented in two ways so that the guests can easily calculate the amount due to them and the price they are paying. The customers can see the rate they have to pay to purchase £1. At the same time they are told the amount they will receive in return for a round amount of their own currency. Exchange rates for major currencies are displayed in the reception area, or cashier's office (*see* Fig. 7.11).

	EXCHANGE RATES		
	£1		££
	=		
Austrian Schillings	20.57	100 Sch.	4.86
Belgian Francs	61.01	100 BF	1.63
French Francs	9.79	10 FF	1.02
German Deutschmarks	2.93	10 DM	3.41
Italian Lire	2125.00	10 000 Lire	4.70
Spanish Pesetas	201.00	1 000 Pes.	4.97
Swiss Francs	2.44	10 SF	4.10
US Dollars	1.60	10 $	6.25

Fig. 7.11 Exchange rates

Hotels will only change notes, because coins would be too costly to transport and handle. A few hotels follow the convention of the banks and issue a receipt quoting each transaction, the guest's room number, and the exchange rate. This has two advantages; if an error is made, the guest can be re-contacted; secondly, as all exchange transactions are recorded, it is easy to balance the amount of foreign currency to be paid in, and thus eliminate to risk of fraud by the operating cashier. Hotel security staff often check against fraud by carrying out spot checks, and making test exchanges with marked currency.

Hotels which operate a computerised system frequently incorporate the updated exchange rates within the front office program. This facilitates the more complex transactions such as part payment of account in foreign currency, and lessons the likelihood of errors occurring.

Petty cash and paid outs

PETTY CASH

Taxi fares, laundry and dry cleaning and other small items are often paid by the cashiers' department from a separate petty cash float. This float is reimbursed daily from the hotel's income and individual petty cash vouchers are allowed against the day's takings. It is important for the control of the petty cash float that only authorised payments are made against receipts for the amount spent. Petty cash payments are subject to an upper limit, and only paid out after being countersigned by a member of the management (*see* Fig. 7.12).

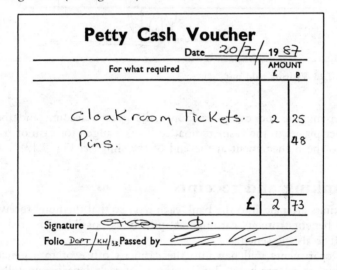

Fig. 7.12 Petty cash voucher

VISITORS' PAID OUT (VPOs)

This is a payment made on behalf of the guest, and is usually only done by prior arrangement which ensures that the client has in fact ordered the payment to be made. A guest may authorise the cashier to pay out a sum of money for an airline ticket that is being delivered to the hotel. Disbursements are also subject to an upper limit as a guard against fraud: they are not allowed to be posted onto the bills of chance guests. Whe posting VPOs it should be remembered that they are exempt of VAT. Whenever possible a VPO, like a petty cash voucher, should be accompanied by a receipt. It should then be signed by the guest or the person

119

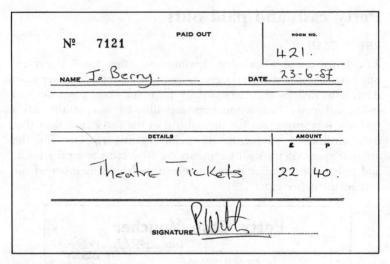

Fig. 7.13 Visitors paid out

receiving the money, posted onto the guest's account and then either placed in the cashiers float to be exchanged for cash or paid in to the management at the end of the shift (*see* Fig. 7.13).

Banking and receipts

Takings are paid into the bank each day, so that the hotel receives full benefit from its earnings as quickly as possible. The risk of theft is also lessened.

Departments will pay into the cashier's office or to a general cashier in a large hotel. The paying-in of each department will be summarised on an internal paying-in slip which can be checked for control purposes. These paying-in slip are split into two sections, detailing UK and foreign takings (*see* Fig. 7.14). These departmental takings are then consolidated for paying into the bank.

A paying-in book is used to record the amount banked each day. The book is usually duplicate, one copy being paid in with the banking, and the other remaining in the book for control purposes. Cash is sorted into denominations and currencies. Coins are bagged, and notes are sorted so that they all face the same way. This 'facing' speeds paying-in at the bank. All banking is entered into the paying-in book. Cheques are listed individually, with the name of the drawer and the amount. A separate page is

Department _____			Date _____		
Machine reading _____			Shift _____		
			Cashier _____		

	Foreign			Sterling	
Amount	Currency	Sterling Equivalent	Amount		
	U.S. Trav. Chq.			£50	
	U.S. notes			£20	
	Other Trav. Chq.			£10	
	Notes			£ 5	
				£ 1	
				Coin	
				£ Trav. Chq.	
				Personal Chq.	
				Petty Cash	
	Total £			**Total**	
				+ Foreign total	
				Grand total	

Fig. 7.14 Department paying in slip

used for foreign currency, and another page for bank credit cards. Foreign currency is calculated at the current exchange rate, and the surplus is often transferred to a foreign exchange account. Group hotels will use a triplicate paying-in book, and send one copy of the stamped paying-in slip to head office to enable central co-ordination of income to be carried out.

The amount of money banked each day is the final link in the circle of control that should operate in the hotel. Because the amount banked is verified by an external source (the bank cashier) it completes the checking procedure. This is shown in the diagram (*see* Fig. 7.15) which outlines the way in which the various sections of the hotel's business are brought together. The control office or a member of management will check each day to ensure

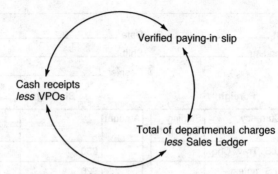

Fig. 7.15 Circle of control of income

that these figures agree. If they do not, then an investigation has to be carried out to find the discrepancy.

RECEIPTS

Guests who pay by cash or cheque upon a departure will be given a receipt by the hotel. The system in use will depend upon the billing method of the hotel. Machine accounting systems normally have a 'paid' function which will automatically receipt the bill as the guest checks out. Manual systems of billing will either use a separate receipt book, or a 'paid' rubber stamp. A receipt book is preferable, for the hotel can keep a tight check on the number of receipts issued and the amount of each one. Receipts normally include the name of the payer and details, amount received in words and figures, the date and signature of the cashier.

Some patented systems of receipting automatically prepare a paying-in summary for the cashier and at the same time issue a baggage clearance, or luggage pass, for the Hall Porter. If this

Fig. 7.16 Luggage pass

122

system is not is used the luggage pass is usually issued by the cashier as the client settles the account (*see* Fig. 7.16). Chance guests who are asked to pay a deposit will be issued with a receipt in the normal way, and the credit will be raised as the first item on the bill.

RECEIPTS FROM OTHER DEPARTMENTS

The cashier is usually responsible for accepting and recording money taken from other sales points, and may also be responsible for reading and checking the tills.

When money is paid in from another cash taking area (e.g. bar, restaurant, telephone etc.) the cash should first be counted and checked against the accompanying slip. A receipt should be issued and given to the member of staff, the money placed in the drawer or till and the details recorded according to the system in use in the hotel.

ADVANCE DEPOSITS AND PRE-PAYMENTS

These are particular popular in resort hotels where guests may book a substantial length of time ahead. The system varies slightly from one hotel to another, but usually involves the following tasks.

1 A receipt is made out and sent to the client;
2 The amount of the deposit is recorded in the diary (or the equivalent record);
3 The deposit is recorded in the Advance Deposit Ledger;
4 On arrival (or departure) the guest's account is credited with the deposit.

Some hotels adopt a system of raising a credit bill for the guest by making a cash posting for the amount of the deposit. This is not very satisfactory since the bill will become very untidy, and may easily be lost or mislaid before the guest's arrival

REFUNDS

Occasionally it may be necessary to refund money to a guest, usually because they have paid in advance and have to leave earlier than planned. The bill will carry a credit balance and the usual way of dealing with this is to obtain a VPO for the amount of the refund and post the VPO to the guest's account, thus reducing the total bill to zero. The guest may be given the cash and asked to sign the voucher which can then be treated in the usual way.

Rapid/speedy check out

Many hotels have introduced this facility as an extra service for those clients who want to make a 'quick getaway' on departure.

It is essential to ensure that the client is made aware of the facility, and some hotels leave notification of the service in the room, while others advise guests at the check in point.

The client may be invited to fill out a card giving permission for the hotel to charge the entire account to the guest's credit card. The card has space for the guest's signature, name, room number and credit card number, or alternatively the cashier may just take an imprint of an acceptable credit card. Since the cashier has plenty of time the normal checks regarding floor limit or lost/stolen cards can be carried out without the degree of urgency associated with the early morning rush.

When the clients leave they need only to deposit the card in a special box, or in the key drop, and the account is finalised in their absence. The hotel will undertake to send a copy of the bill and the credit card voucher to the client (*see* Fig. 7.17).

NAME ______________ MR/MRS

ROOM NUMBER ______________

CARD: ACCESS ☐ VISA ☐ AMEX ☐ DINERS ☐ THF ☐ JCB ☐

NUMBER ☐☐☐☐☐☐☐☐☐☐☐☐☐☐☐☐

EXPIRY DATE ______________

DATE OF DEPARTURE: ______________

Address to which account copy should be sent:
(CAPITALS)

....

....

....

If settling your account by Credit Card we invite you to take advantage of our rapid check-out facility. On departure simply complete the details and place this card with your key at the key drop on the reception desk.

A copy of your account together with your credit card voucher will be sent to you on your day of departure.

Our receptionists will be delighted to make any onward hotel reservations within Trusthouse Forte in the U.K. or worldwide.

I hereby agree that my credit card should be used to settle the full amount of my bill and sent to the stated address.

Signature ....

Fig. 7.17 Rapid check-out

Safe deposit facilities

Liability for loss of guest's property can be limited through the Hotel Proprietors Act 1956 (*see* Chapter 2) if safe custody is offered for valuables and money.

The two common methods of offering this safe custody are deposit envelopes, which are stored in a large safe, and individual deposit boxes.

DEPOSIT ENVELOPES

The guest is offered a strong envelope into which they seal their property and sign over the seal. The cashier marks the envelope with the guest's name and room number, and issues a receipt for the envelope.

The receipt is countersigned by the guest and the receipt number is noted on the envelope, which is deposited in the safe with other property. The receipt is issued for a 'sealed envelope'. By doing this, the cashier is relieved of the task of counting sums of money, or agreeing an inventory of contents with the guest.

When the guest requests the return of the property they pass over the receipt and sign in the receipt book for the return of the envelope with the seal intact. The cashier verifies the guest's signature against the original and clips the receipt back into the receipt book. The book in this way is evidence of a completed transaction. A quick control check can be made by counting the envelopes in the safe and comparing the number with the number of receipts currently issued. Although this is a secure system, it does mean that a new envelope has to be used for each transaction, even if a guest only wishes to remove part of their property from the deposit. A similar system adopts two-part receipts which are attached to especially printed envelopes stored in the cashier's office (*see* Fig. 7.18).

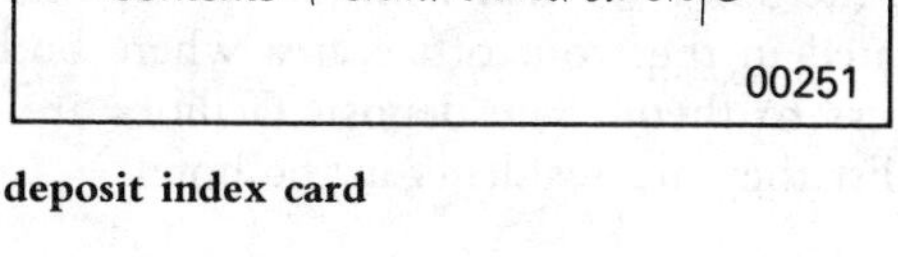

```
Date 23/6              Room 716

Guest name Mr. G. Sparrow


Contents 1 brown sealed envelope

                                          00251
```

Fig. 7.18 Safe deposit index card

SAFE DEPOSIT BOX

Larger hotels utilise individual deposit boxes for property. The individual boxes are large enough to take personal property such as jewellery, passports, money and travellers cheques. Larger items such as briefcases, or even fur coats, have to be separately stored. The boxes are stored in individual safes which are secured by two locks. The first lock is opened by a key which is common

SAFE DEPOSIT INDEX CARD		Room No.	Box. No.
Guest(s) Name(s) Finch Mrs C .		709	12
Address 10 Central Parade, Welwyn. Herts.			

Important/Please read carefully conditions set out overleaf, and sign in space provided.

This section to be completed each time contents of safe box are withdrawn:-

Date	Time	Signature(s)	Receptionist
23/6	15.30	O. Finch.	eKo

Section below to be completed when guest(s) release(s) possession of said box

I/We hereby acknowledge receipt of the contents of safe box number.....................
and release possession of said box

Receptionist

....

Date.....................Time...................Guest(s) Signature(s).......................

Fig. 7.19 Safe deposit index card

to every safe; this key is held by the cashier. The second lock has an individual key, which is issued to the guest who signs the deposit slip (*see* Fig. 7.19). The safe can only be opened when both keys are in the locks. The guest and the cashier must also be present. Each time a guest wishes to remove property he signs the slip. The cashier countersigns to authorise the guest's signature, and the box is opened with the two keys. These deposit boxes are located in the front office area where both guests and staff have access to them. Safe deposit facilities are only offered to people whilst they are residents in the hotel.

Self-assessment questions

1 What dictates the size of the float?
2 Name six methods of payment.
3 List four functions of a cashier.
4 What is meant by liquidity?
5 What is meant by rapid/speedy checkout?
6 Show how income is controlled.
7 Explain one system of handling safe deposits.

Chapter 8
TOURS AND GROUPS

Chapter objectives

After studying this chapter you should be able to:
- identify the influences on the price that can be charged for accommodation to a tour;
- show how an inclusive tour is packaged and sold to travel agents;
- explain the special needs of the conference organiser and how they can be met.

An increasingly important source of business for hotels is the package tour, or group. The minimum size for group status is normally five rooms, but with increases in transport carrying facilities, a group can often be as large as 100 or more rooms.

Not all groups are holidaymakers. They may also be conference delegates, travelling sports teams, or business people attending a trade fair. The main characteristic of a group booking is the uniformity of the arrangements. All members will arrive and depart on the same day, and the booking details will be handled by one person.

Pricing and selling

The rate the hotel charges a group for rooms will depend upon a number of factors. The key points that must be considered when quoting rates for a group are:

1 time of year;
2 time of week;
3 length of stay;
4 how many rooms;
5 what other facilities they will use;
6 who they are.

A group booking will benefit from a lower rate if it takes space out of season when the accommodation would otherwise be empty.

Any booking accepted during the high season may result in loss of revenue to the hotel. In accepting a tour at a discount rate the hotel may have to refuse potential guests who would have been happy to pay full rate for their accommodation.

In setting a rate the first point the reception manager will check is the occupancy on the same dates in the previous year. If occupancy was low—beneath 45 per cent—then it is possible to set a low price, for it is unlikely that the hotel will be full when the tour arrives. If the previous year's occupancy was above 80 per cent, then the rate needs to be correspondingly higher.

The time of week that the booking is for is also important. Even in the high season there may be a day or two days when occupancy is significantly lower. For this reason, it is important to check the reservation chart and booking details of previous years extremely carefully. High occupancy levels are achieved by filling in the gaps between the peaks of demand.

NET RATES

Bookings made by travel agents are normally subject to a commission to the agent. When quoting rates for tours, though, most hotels quote a 'net rate' on which there is no commission. An example of how a hotel will set its price to a tour operator is shown in Fig. 8.1. This shows that, sharing a twin room and paying full rate, the guest would spend £34.50 per day. The highest price at which the room can be sold to the agent is £31.05, allowing for a commission of 10%. The hotel must now negotiate a price with the agent which allows both of them to make a profit.

An alternative strategy is to include some meals or other facilities in the package and charge an all-in price (*see* Fig. 8.2) including accommodation, breakfast, and one main meal with wine. If it is out of season then the hotel would be able to reduce its rates both for accommodation and also for food and beverage.

Normal Twin Rate		Tour Rate	
Tariff	60.00	Tariff per ½ twin	34.50
VAT	9.00	Less 10%	3.45
	69.00	NET RATE	31.05
PER PERSON	34.50		

Fig. 8.1 Possible price range for tour booking

½ Twin @	30.70
Table d'hote meu	11.30
Coffee	70
½ carafe wine	5.30
	£48.00

Fig. 8.2 Demi-pension tour cost

The agent could be offered the package at a rate.of, for example, £25.00 net and the hotel would have a substantial contribution to income from each tour member, for the total expenditure is higher than a full rate guest taking room and breakfast only, and also there is no guarantee that a normal guest would use the food and beverage facilities of the hotel.

PACKAGE

If the person buying the accommodation is a travel agent it is possible that they are using the hotel as part of a 'package' that they will market at an all-in price through retail travel agents and brochures.

The travel agent, normally a wholesaler, purchases aircraft seats, coaches for transfers, hotel accommodation, restaurant meals and other goods and services, sets the price for the package and has a brochure printed.

By buying in large quantities, the agent is able to negotiate prices that are cheaper than those available to the individual travelling alone.

The agent is also able to offer the tour passengers security. The traveller will not have to negotiate with taxi drivers, hotels, porters and restaurants for each part of his or her holiday. For many people who are not used to travelling, especially in a foreign country, this is an important benefit.

SELLING

To sell accommodation to the tour operator the hotel will be working with a lead time of between twelve and eighteen months before the arrival of the guests.

The aims of the tour operator and the hotelier are conflicting in handling accommodation sales. The agent wishes to buy space in the hotel in peak season at the cheapest possible rate. On the other hand, the hotel hopes to sell space off-peak at the highest rate possible.

To reconcile these aims some hoteliers and tour operators have developed a 'series' of packages. The tour operator is offered peak accommodation at a discount rate provided that they also take an agreed amount of off-peak accommodation. This is often negotiated as a fixed relationship. For each room the tour operator books in an off-peak period the hotel will offer two rooms in peak season at a discount.

A variation of this is where the tour operator is offered accommodation on a sliding scale price, dependent upon the total amount booked in the year.

Figure 8.3 shows that the tour operator is offered the first 500 room nights at £45 the next 500 at £28 and so on. The steps down encourage the operator to promote the hotel (or chain) because they receive a larger discount as they place more business with the hotel. If the operator places 2500 room nights with a hotel, the average rate falls to £10 on a room that has a tariff rate of £30. The tour operator can either pass on this discount in lower prices, or use it to increase their profit.

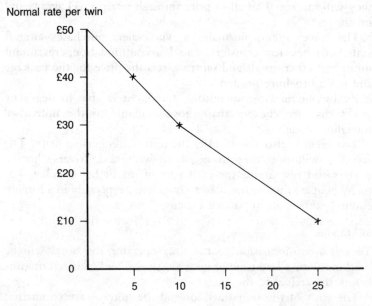

Fig. 8.3 Price/volume relation

Complimentary rooms are normally offered by the hotel to the courier or tour leader of groups, although there is normally a minimum group size qualification on this facility.

Booking

Because of the long lead time of tour bookings, there is often a large difference between the number of rooms originally booked and the number that are finally taken.

The reception manager can use previous records to assess the amount they need to overbook to compensate for this high cancellation figure. Large hotels will often specify the percentage of rooms that they will allocate to tours and groups. This is particularly useful for luxury hotels who may be worried about their image and consequently only allow 20 per cent of their rooms to be let to tours at any one time. Other hotels will have 80 per cent of their guests on package tours and plan the services to meet this market requirement.

CANCELLATION DEADLINE

As a protection against last minute cancellations of large amounts of space, a system of cancellation deadlines is used. This formalises the arrangements for cancelling rooms. Normally the deadline will fall four weeks before the arrival date, but for large groups this can be extended to up to three months. Before the deadline date the reception manager sends the tour operator a reminder of the tour arrival date, length of stay, and number of rooms. The operator has to return this with any amendments by the deadline date. If the number of rooms is reduced after this time then the hotel can charge full non-arrival rates for all the rooms not taken up.

BOOKING FORM

To ensure that all arrangements are clearly detailed a special tour booking form is used. This establishes full details of the group and their requirements at the hotel. When taking the booking the reception manager can use the form as a sales aid to maximise the tour's use of the hotel.

Figure 8.4 shows a tour booking form. It is more complex than a usual reservation form. The exact arrival and departure time for a group is important as it will affect the staffing requirements of the hotel on the day. Where the group is arriving from may also be important. If the group is arriving early in the morning from

		Unit				Date

Tour operator _____ Group name _____

Telephone _____

Telex _____

Contact _____

Rooms	No.	Net rate			Arrival	Departure
SB			Date			
TB			Time			
DB			From			
Other			To			

Special requirements_____

_____

Meals		Day of arrival Date __	Day 2 Date __	Day 3 Date __	Day 4 Date __
	Breakfast				
	Lunch				
	Dinner				
	Function				

Subject to terms and conditions overleaf

Fig. 8.4 Tour booking form

the USA there will be a time change, and the guests will want to obtain their rooms as quickly as possible. On the day of departure, rooms are normally vacated by midday, but the group may not be leaving the hotel until 6 p.m.

BOOKING DETAILS

All other details of the booking must be clarified with the agent before the group arrives. This is especially necessary concerning payment of extras, honouring of personal cheques, foreign exchange facilities, and tips for hotel staff.

In quoting a rate to a tour operator the hotel will normally establish whether the courier or tour leader will pay 'baggage money' to the porters, or whether it is to be included in the rate quoted. Attention to minor points of this nature will ensure that the stay of the group is trouble free.

ROOMING LIST

At the deadline date the tour operator will confirm the final details of arrival and departure and the number of rooms, and will also send to the hotel a rooming list. This will show all the full names of the tour members and also who is sharing twin rooms, and any special requests (such as adjacent rooms). The rooming list may also include pre-registration information concerning passport numbers, addresses and nationality of all the guests. The hotel may then be able to pre-register all the members of the party.

Handling and billing

The arrival of any group of people together will always place a strain upon the staff of the reception desk. As the reception is aware of the time of arrival of the group and details of the rooms required, the maximum amount of advance preparation can be undertaken.

All departments are notified of the size and arrival details of the tour through the ten-day forecast. When the tour actually arrives the receptionist should begin by checking the rooming list with the courier to ensure that there have been no late cancellations, or alterations in the room types.

REGISTRATION

There are three alternative methods of handling the tour registration. The first is to obtain all details of the group from the operator in advance, and to dispense completely with individual registration cards. This method is quick and cuts down paperwork. The drawbacks to this method are lack of confirmation that information provided by the operator is correct, and also the lack of signatures of the individual members; this could cause problems in the verification of charges signed to guest rooms.

The second method is to provide the tour leader with registration cards for each guest, which are completed *en route* to the hotel. As the guests arrive the cards are handed to the receptionist in exchange for the room key. Key cards will usually have been prepared in advance and will be given out at this stage.

The third method is to register guests in the normal way as they arrive at the hotel. This often causes congestion around the reception desk, to the detriment of other hotel guests, although this can be alleviated by the setting up of a special desk/table just for the tour members.

ROOM ALLOCATION

If the group is large the allocation of rooms may present some problems. Midday arrival will probably mean that all the rooms are not ready, so the reception department will have to keep some guests waiting to gain access to their rooms. The allocation of rooms can be organised to place all the tour members as near together as possible. Luggage distribution is simplified by doing this, but an uneven strain may be placed upon one section of the housekeeping department.

The porter's desk will be responsible for providing parking space for the coach, the distribution of mail and messages to the guests and the speedy distribution of the guests' luggage. On arrival, the bags are carried in, and the total number agreed with the tour leader. Tips may be based upon the number of bags, and the total also acts as a check when bags are brought down on the day of departure. Reception should finally check that a key is available for every room before it is allocated to the new guest.

GUEST CHARGES

When booking, the tour operator will have clarified what charges they will be responsible for, and those that the guests will pay themsevles.

Charges are posted onto an 'extras' bill for each guest. The bill office staff have to be clearly informed of the breakdown of charges, especially for meals where guests may be charged individually for alcoholic beverages, but coffee and tea may be the responsibility of the tour operator.

The main bill or master account will be charged daily with accommodation and food and beverage charges to ensure that posted charges are a true reflection of the business done on that day.

CHECK OUT

On the day of departure the reception department has to ensure that all extra bills are paid, all keys returned and the baggage cleared before the group departs.

If a tour is leaving later than midday, a hospitality room may be offered to the group. This is a large guest room easily accessible from the lobby of the hotel. Tour guests may use the room to rest, store hand luggage and utilise bathroom facilities before they finally depart. A hospitality room is a courtesy that is much appreciated by tour guests; the hotel also benefits from its use by gaining access to all the guest rooms for servicing by the maids.

The tour leader will give the reception manager a voucher itemising all the charges the tour company will be responsible for, and counter-signed by him.

BILLING

A copy of the voucher will have been sent to the hotel with the final rooming list. Both of these vouchers are attached to the hotel account which is completed, checked and authorised by the reception manager and sent to the tour operator for payment. Payment terms are agreed before the tour arrives, for unlike a normal ledger bill, tour bills can often total several thousand pounds in larger hotels. Credit status is checked by the hotel before any bookings are accepted, and also an agreement for handling disputes over the account is established. This will not only minimise bad debt provision but also guard against the tour operator holding up payment of the total bill while a minor dispute is resolved.

Conferences

Conferences, conventions, seminars, exhibitions and workshops are frequently held in hotels that have meeting room facilities.

The prime purpose for the customer is the meeting itself. The use of bedrooms and food and beverage facilities is of secondary importance. What the organiser is interested in is a package of facilities that will meet all of his or her needs satisfactorily.

The reception department has to be fully aware of the other facilities of the hotel and their capabilities, if this specialised market is to be met.

MEETING ROOMS

An accurate plan of every meeting room in the hotel should exist. The plan must include details of all the mains services and other facilities, but it should be clear enough to be read and understood by a person without architectural training.

The main points in the plan are:

1 full dimensions of the room (including ceiling height);
2 location of entrances and exits; and their size;

135

3 position of dividing doors;
4 location of pillars and other obstructions;
5 power points and loading;
6 gas points and pressure;
7 water points and pressure;
8 floor type and loading limit;
9 lighting and capability;
10 air conditioning.

The basic information about the room should be supplemented with an inventory of aids to conference presentation. These normally include:

1 film projection facilities;
2 microphone and amplifiers;
3 overhead projectors;
4 lecterns and staging;
5 slide projectors;
6 translation facilities.

Roving microphones and simultaneous translation facilities are only likely to be found in the largest purpose built conference hotels, but even the smallest hotel will benefit from an inventory of blackboards, flip charts and other equipment.

Seating layouts and plans can also be prepared so that conference organisers may make a choice between the various alternatives; coupled with this should be a knowledge of the capacity of every room in any layout, and advice on the most suitable room for a particular function.

Over a period of time the hotel can build up a folio of photographs of the room in various layouts from previous meetings. These photographs can be a very useful sales aid when meeting conference organisers.

FOOD AND BEVERAGE FACILITIES

In selling meeting space, the reception will need to be in close contact with the food and beverage department in order to organise details of meals, snacks and coffee breaks. An effective conference or meeting relies upon accurate timing at all stages and this is essential in the provision of meals. Food and beverage staff are able to assist enormously by serving food swiftly. This may perhaps help conference planners to make up time lost in a session through a seminar overrunning.

ROOM FACILITIES

The reception department will naturally have a full inventory of all guest rooms in the hotel. Organisers of conferences will be particularly interested in the rooms for the VIPs and rooms that will also be used for cocktail parties or entertaining.

If possible these should be shown set up for a cocktail party and an explanation given of the signposting and direction facilities offered by the hotel.

Rates should be agreed with the conference organiser along with rates for extra night accommodation and extra beds. Conference visitors can often be encouraged to stay over a weekend with special rates. As with a tour, the position of deadlines, room guarantees and extra bills has to be settled before the delegates arrive.

CONFERENCE BACK-UP

In many instances the hotel will have more experience of conference organisation than the person buying the facilities.

This expertise can be used as a sales aid in guiding the conference organiser. Proposals can be made about registration facilities, name tags for delegates, menus and give aways. The hotel can also assist in the printing of schedules, delegate lists, and speeches. If the conference is also being attended by delegates' spouses, then the hotel may be able to propose alternative social arrangements while meetings are in progress.

TO SUCCEED

Successful conference hotels have realised that organisers have two needs foremost in their minds.

The first is the desire to deal with one person for all the arrangements, so the hotel should put together a package that can be quoted at an all-in price per delegate. The traditional practice of acting as an agent for florists, photographers and projection hire firms and adding their charges to the bill has been superseded by the specialist conference planner, who can deal direct with the client.

A conference checklist that assists the organiser and also acts as a sales aid is shown in Fig. 8.5.

The second need is generally automatically satisfied at the same time as the first (but the recognition of it by hotel personnel can be an invaluable sales tool). The conference organiser wants security, and reassurance. If the meeting is a failure, a large part of the blame will be placed upon him or her. The hotel must set out to reassure the organiser that the meeting will be a success, and that it will run smoothly and on time.

Dates		Meeting	
Accommodation	☐	Floor plans	☐
Meeting rooms	☐	Timing	☐
Organisers	☐	Seating	☐
		Hand-outs	☐
Rooms		Paper/pencils	☐
		Water	☐
No. of each type	☐	Ashtrays	☐
Syndicate	☐	Waste bins	☐
Function	☐		
Press	☐		
Storage	☐		
Rates	☐	**Food and beverage**	
		Coffee	☐
VIP Guests		Tea	☐
		Bar	☐
Tickets	☐	Lunch	☐
Transport	☐	Dinner	☐
Name plaques	☐	Function	☐
		Breakfast	☐
Equipment		Charge facilities	☐
Signs	☐		
Lighting	☐		
Staging	☐	**Other**	
Sound	☐		
Projection	☐	Press notices	☐
Display	☐	Advertising	☐
Flowers	☐	Security	☐
Music	☐	Entertainment	☐
Special Eqpt.	☐	Garage	☐
Tape recording	☐	Photographer	☐

Fig. 8.5 Conference checklist

Hotels that recognise these needs and systematically set out to satisfy them are successful in the conference and meeting market.

Self-assessment questions

1 List four factors that will affect the price quoted for a tour.
2 Explain what a net rate is.
3 Draw a flowchart of a tour booking.
4 Show the different systems for registering tours.
5 Prepare a room inventory for a hotel that wishes to handle conferences.
6 Draw up a checklist for conference organisers.
7 What points should be checked before a package tour finally leaves the hotel?

Chapter 9
STATISTICS AND REPORTS

Chapter objectives

After studying this chapter you should be able to:
- distinguish the various methods of calculating and measuring business performance;
- identify the various operational reports that are produced in the front office and show their purpose and relevance.

Business statistics

Statistics are an extremely useful method of identifying how the business is doing. The presentation of information in a standardised form makes comparison and interpretation simpler for management.

It is possible to compare actual performance against projected performance and to make internal comparisons—this year against last year, one shift against another, and so on.

OCCUPANCY

The most common and effective statistic in a hotel is the level of occupancy. Most hotels in the UK derive the bulk of their turnover (and profits) from the sale of accommodation. It is essential that management has an accurate, up-to-date picture of the occupancy of their unit.

Occupancy is usually expressed as a percentage. By using the percentage it is possible to make meaningful comparisons. Income alone, for example, is unreliable, for while a hotel may be taking more than the previous year, there is no allowance for any increases in prices that may have occurred.

There are three normal methods of calculating occupancy. These are:

1 room;
2 sleeper or bed;
3 income.

The best way of showing how they differ and how they are calculated is to use the following example:

Hotel   50 single rooms
          25 twin rooms
          25 double rooms

Total   100

Tariff: £50.00 per person per night.

All rooms are let with one person in each room paying a discount rate of £40 per person.

$$\text{Room occupancy} = \frac{\text{rooms sold}}{\text{total rooms}} \times \frac{100}{1} = \frac{100}{100} \times \frac{100}{1}$$

So the room occupancy is 100 per cent. At first glance the hotel is doing very well.

$$\text{Sleeper occupancy} = \frac{\text{no. of sleepers}}{\text{total poss. sleepers}} \times \frac{100}{1} = \frac{100}{150} \times \frac{100}{1}$$

The sleeper occupancy is only 67 per cent.

Bed occupancy is sometimes used as a term instead of sleeper occupancy, but confusion can arise through the existence of double beds in the hotel, which although they count as one bed can sleep two people.

$$\text{Income occupancy} = \frac{\text{actual income}}{\text{total poss. income}} \times \frac{100}{1} = \frac{400}{750} \times \frac{100}{1}$$

The income occupancy is just 53 per cent. This is partly due to the discount on the normal rate, but also reflects the poor letting strategy of having only one person in each room. So, although all the rooms in the hotel are let, it is only earning just over half of its potential.

The method chosen by the hotel to calculate its occupancy level is obviously very important. The most accurate picture is given by the income occupancy figure. This shows clearly that 47 per cent of the hotel's potential income on this particular night is lost. The transient nature of the hotel's 'product', or 'bed nights', means that there is no opportunity to recoup the revenue lost.

Income occupancy of 100 per cent is very rarely achieved even by the most successful hotels, because a room is often unavailable due to maintenance, or discounts are given to tour operators or airline personnel on the normal tariff rate. For this reason, the most common measure adopted is the sleeper occupancy, which is more likely to reach 100 per cent.

Sleeper occupancy also reflects more accurately the ability of the reception staff, for they are rarely involved in the setting of tour rates or discounts.

All occupancy figures can be further refined by calculating them on the basis of 'available sleepers'. If ten rooms are unavailable due to redecoration, then the hotel rooms are reduced by this number.

$$\text{Available room occupancy} = \frac{\text{no. of rooms sold}}{\text{rooms available}} \times \frac{100}{1}$$

Using the earlier example of a 100-room hotel, if 90 rooms are let occupancy would be shown as 90 per cent, but if ten rooms are unavailable due to redecoration, then available occupancy would be 100 per cent

$$\left(\frac{90}{90} \times \frac{100}{1} \right)$$

Clearly, the reception cannot do better than this.

This is fairer on the reception department, for they are not able to sell rooms that are not available to be let, so it shows their efforts more accurately. Some large units compromise by showing the figures for both total occupancy and available occupancy.

The maximum occupancy level that can be achieved is not 100 per cent. It can sometimes be higher. This can occur in two ways. Firstly, extra beds that are not used in calculating the occupancy may be utilised during busy periods. Secondly, 'transient' hotels (particularly at airports) may let a room more than once during a 24 hour period.

DOUBLE OCCUPANCY

Another occupancy measure frequently calculated is the number of double rooms sold as doubles. This also is a very accurate measure of the skill of the reservation clerks.

The most common method of calculating double occupancy is:

$$\frac{\text{no. of double rooms let as doubles}\star}{\text{total number of doubles}} \times \frac{100}{1}$$

$\star$ this refers to twin rooms as well as large bedded rooms.

Example

hotel	let	1 person
	2 people	10
25D	15	5
25T	20	50
50S	—	
100 rooms		

All rooms are let, but ten doubles and five twins only have one occupant. Double occupancy is $\dfrac{35}{50} \times \dfrac{100}{1} = 70$ per cent.

If the reservation department has accepted too many bookings for single rooms, then the double occupancy percentage will reflect this. The problem that the reservation clerk faces is that if he or she refuses a booking for a single because they are all sold, with a subsequent booking for a double materialise, or will the room remain empty? If accurate occupancy statistics are kept over a period, then the reservation clerk can use them to aid decision making. Some hotels have an intermediate rate for a double room that is only being used by one person. If the normal single rate is £20, and the double rate is £35, then a double for one person will be offered at £30. This would count as two sleepers for calculation of double occupancy statistics.

AVERAGE RATE

The average room rate, or average sleeper rate, is calculated by many chain operated hotels.

$$\text{Average room rate} = \frac{\text{apartment income}}{\text{no. of rooms sold}} = £$$

$$\text{Average sleeper rate} = \frac{\text{apartment income}}{\text{no. of sleepers}} = £$$

In the hotel below, the maximum average rate would be £15.

Hotel
25 twins £20
25 singles £10

If this hotel was let 10 twins @ £20, 15 twins @ £15, and 20 singles @ £10 then apartment income would be £625. Therefore the average room rate would be:

$$\frac{625}{45} = £13.88$$

This shows that some rooms are being let at less than the tariff rate.

Probably the most useful rate in the UK is the average room rate. This can be compared with the theoretical maximum obtainable.

Once again, it is a measure of the performance of the unit. A high average room rate will show that rooms are being sold at the maximum obtainable.

A hotel that has two double beds in a room and caters for families travelling together can let the room to either two, three or four persons.

The extent to which they are maximising the occupancy of each individual room will be shown in a high average room rate. On the other hand, if rooms are being heavily discounted, or given at complimentary rates, the average rate figure will reflect this.

Average rate and income occupancy are similar in their ability to give a very clear picture of the efficiency in financial terms of the rooms department.

OCCUPANCY REPORT

The occupancy figures and other information is presented daily to the management and is consolidated on a standard occupancy report. This is either prepared by the late shift on reception or (in larger hotels) will be prepared by the night audit staff.

Figure 9.1 shows a typical occupancy report for a large city centre hotel. Room types are shown individually to show how rooms are let and which are the most popular. Discounts and complimentary are listed separately so that management can ensure that all reductions have been authorised and see from what source they come. Occupancy information is presented both in room figure and also as a percentage where possible. The number of reservations for the day is shown as 100 per cent so that cancellations and 'no shows' can be expressed as a percentage of reservations. This assists planning for overbooking levels. Apartment income is cross checked against the amount posted to guest bills. Out of order (O/O/O) rooms of each type are shown in the report. Occupancy this night last year is a quick guide to show how the hotel is progressing. Special events—exhibitions, conferences and also public holidays are listed, for they will affect the occupancy level that the hotel has been able to achieve.

Occupancy report

Day	
Date	
Unit	

Room type	Total rooms	O/O/O	Let	Vacant
Single Twin Double Suite Other				
Total				

Discounts and complimentary

Number of rooms	Rate	Name	Affiliation

	%
Total rooms	100
O/O/O	
Available	
Vacant	
Let	
Sleepers	
Double occupancy	
Reservations	100
Cancellations	
No shows	

Apartment income

Average room rate £

Occupancy week to date

Occupancy this night last year

Special events ....
....
....

Prepared by_____

Fig. 9.1 Occupancy report

Guest statistics

The previous statistics have been concerned with the hotel as a whole, and how successful it is. Another group of statistics that are commonly collected relate to the customers who use the hotel and their characteristics.

LENGTH OF GUEST STAY

The average guest stay will affect a number of decisions in the hotel. These concern mainly staffing levels and rotas, facilities offered, and even the number of towels placed in guest rooms.

There are two ways of calculating the average guest stay; these are the mean average and the modal average.

$$\text{Mean average Guest stay} = \frac{\text{no. of sleeper nights sold}}{\text{no. of guests}}$$

The period used for calculating this is generally one month. Normally the figure will not be an exact number of nights, so many hotels will talk of their average guest stay being 2.65 nights, which, although useful, is not clear.

An alternative to this is to produce a statistic which shows the most common length of stay. Obviously, no guest stays for 2.65 nights.

The table below shows the number of nights spent in a hotel by 200 guests:

Length of stay	No. of guests
1 night	40
2 nights	80
3 nights	30
4 nights	20
5 nights	20
6 nights	10

From this, it can be seen that the most common length of stay is two nights. Eighty guests stayed for two nights. This average is called the 'mode'. It is the most commonly occurring figure in the group. The number of nights stayed can be easily logged from departure cards or paid bills.

With this information, it is also possible to calculate the mean average. This is shown in the table on p. 147.

145

Mkt. Type Persons		For Office Use	
	SURNAME	Room Number	
	FORENAME	Arrival Date	
	HOME ADDRESS	No. of Nights	
		Rate (£)	
	Account to be settled by: Cash ☐ Voucher ☐ Credit Card ☐	Remarks	
	Nationality	Car Reg. Number	
Name	OVERSEAS VISITORS	Signature	
	Passport Number		
Dept. Date	Issued at		Receptionist
	Next destination		

RETURN VISITS			
Date	Room	Nts	Rate

Fig. 9.2 Registration details as an aid to marketing

146

Length of stay	No. of guests	Guest nights (1 × 2)
1 night	40	40
2 nights	80	160
3 nights	30	90
4 nights	20	80
5 nights	20	100
6 nights	10	60
	200	530

By dividing 200 into 530, the average stay of 2.65 nights is found. So, although the mean average is 2.65 nights, over half the guests stay for two nights or less.

GUEST ORIGIN

Effective marketing begins with knowledge of the customer. Hotels are able to find out more about their customers by reference to registration details (*see* Fig 9.2).

Hotels which operate a computerised system will ensure that this information is readily available as part of the program. Those hotels which still operate a traditional system will find the information more laborious to collect, but essential to ensure maximum occupancy is obtained.

Nationality of guests can be easily logged and presented every three months as a percentage of total guests: This can also be done

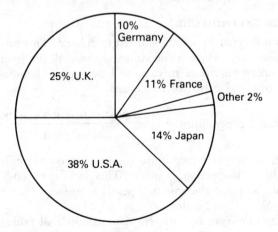

Fig. 9.3 Pie chart of guest nationality

147

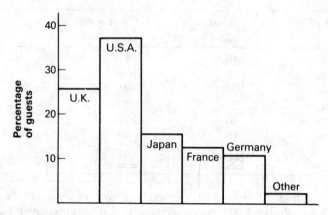

Fig. 9.4 Histogram of guest nationality

for UK guests by area or county. The simplest method is to present the number of guests from each country as a percentage of the total. Greater accuracy is produced by showing the guest nights produced by each group as a percentage of the total. For ease of interpretation, these figures are usually presented in a pie chart (*see* Fig. 9.3) or a histogram (*see* Fig. 9.4).

A separate chart can be produced for the regions that UK guests come from, if they constitute a major section of the hotel's business.

This information can be used in the planning of sales campaigns or advertising expenditure, or perhaps in the recruiting of staff with special language skills.

AVERAGE EXPENDITURE

The amount spent by guests is often calculated. This can only be done effectively where expenditure is posted on to a guest's account. Any purchases in cash will be recorded under chance business of the department concerned.

$$\text{Average expenditure} = \frac{\text{total posted to guest's account}}{\text{no. of guests}}$$

A simple average expenditure figure can become more useful if a further classification is made. This can be expenditure per nationality and also the amount spent by business sources (travel agents, businessmen, tour guests etc.).

The amount spent by different nationalities will probably vary substantially. The information can be presented along with the

148

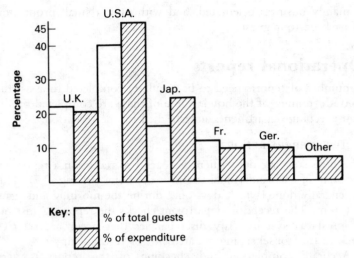

Fig. 9.5 Guest nationality and expenditure

histogram of nationalities; in this way it is easy to compare the information.

Figure 9.5 shows that although Japanese guests are responsible for 14% of guest nights, they produced 25 per cent of the income. Their expenditure was markedly higher than UK guests.

SOURCE OF BOOKINGS

The source of bookings can be useful in planning for the hotel. Classification can be either by number of reservations, or by number of room nights. Fig. 9.6 shows a profile of a hotel that

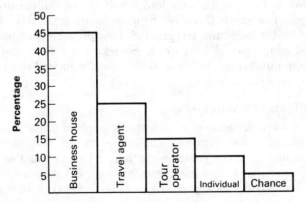

Fig. 9.6 Source of booking in city centre hotel

149

is mainly business orientated, and with only a small proportion of package tour guests.

Operational reports

A number of reports need to be regularly completed to assist the smooth running of the hotel. Some of these are completed by the housekeeping department, and checked by the reception.

HOUSEKEEPERS REPORT

The housekeeping department will send to reception a report on the state of each individual room in the hotel (*see* Fig. 9.7). This is generally done twice a day, once during the morning and again at 6 p.m. The reception department checks the report against the room status system. Any discrepancies that occur are referred back to the housekeeping department for re-checking.

Accurate completion and checking of the report is very important, especially in large hotels. If the housekeeper's report shows 'vacant', and the room status system shows 'let', it may be that a guest has changed rooms, or even left without settling their account. Failure by the reception staff to follow this up may mean loss of revenue to the hotel. There are many other ways in which the hotel may be losing money, such as only charging one guest when there are two in a room. It is not just the completion of the housekeeper's report that is important, but equally necessary is the checking of all the queries that arise from it.

INCIDENT BOOK/HANDOVER BOOK

A log is often kept to ensure the smooth handover from one shift to another. In this, the shift leader will record information and any special incidents that have happened during the day. This is signed by the incoming receptionist. Lost property that has been handed in and passed over to the housekeeper may be noted, or the room numbers of guests who have been requested to pay their bills up to date.

STANDARD ROOM REPORT

The reception department is sometimes involved in the filling out of standard room reports. These are checks that are made periodically on every room in the hotel. The aim of the report is to ensure that the rooms are maintained and decorated to the highest standard. Each part of the room is checked to establish that it is clean, and that all appliances are working. When the

4th Floor				Date				19	
401	VAC	421		438		454	VAC	468	
402	OOQ	423		439		455		469	
403		424		440		456		470	
404	OOQ	425		441		457		471	
406		426		442		461	Suite		
407		427		443		458			
408		428		444		459			
409		429		445		462			
410		430		446		419			
411		431		447					
412		432		449		463			
414		434		450		464			
415		435		451		465			
416		436		452		466			
420		437		453		467			

Housekeeper's Signature

Fig. 9.7 Housekeeper's report

report has been completed then maintenance requests are made out as required. A standard room report would check furnishings, wall coverings, lights, directories, curtains etc. more thoroughly and systematically than would be possible by a maid during her daily shift.

Forecasts

Forecasting is a task of the reception department that affects other areas of the hotel. Restaurants and other sales outlets will base their expectations of trade on the occupancy forecast produced by reception.

OCCUPANCY FORECAST

A general prediction of occupancy month by month through the year can be made by the reception department. In producing this their main guidelines will be last year's occupancy, the level of advance bookings already made, and an assessment of any changes in the market. A new hotel opening in the same area may reduce occupancy, while an important trade fair may increase it.

FIVE-DAY FORECAST

A more accurate prediction of occupancy is normally produced by reception for the next five days or so (*see* Fig. 9.8). This five-day forecast is done daily, so that the forecast is always updated and extended every 24 hours. It is circulated to relevant departments to aid planning. The forecast will enable the reservations department to accept or reject bookings at short notice and assist the kitchen in buying food for breakfasts and other meals.

Financial reports

Sales figures and turnover will be reported daily to management, but some figures may also be presented as ratios or percentages.

Management by exception is often practised in the assessment of financial statistics. Upper and lower limits are set by management, and no action is taken unless these limits are exceeded. The limit for bad debts may be 0.7 per cent of turnover. Provided that bad debts do not exceed this figure, no action is taken. This form of presentation is easier to interpret than the raw figures.

DAILY TRADING REPORT

A daily total of sales in every department will be made by the front office. This will show not only the amount spent in each department, but also some measure of activity, such as the number of covers at lunch and dinner. Fig. 9.9 shows a simple daily report of income. If a special promotion is being carried out, then its effectiveness can be monitored by presenting the income of each department as a percentage of total takings. A sales campaign may aim to increase floor service sales from 5 per cent of daily takings to 7 per cent, for example.

Unit _____

Date

Day

Today   **Departures**

Overnight vacant

+ Check out today

+ Extra departures

= Available

Arrivals

Reservations

— No shows

Net arrivals

Vacant (short)

Day/Date

Departures

Projected check out

+ Extra departures

Arrivals

Reservation count

— No shows

Net arrivals

Vacant (short)

Prepared by _____

Fig. 9.8 Five-day forecast

153

Income Unit _____

Rooms

Day

£

Occupancy % ☐ ☐ Date

Restaurant covers

Breakfast

Lunch

Dinner

Floor
service

Banqueting

— — — — — — — —

— — — — — — — —

— — — — — — — —

Bar

Sundry services

Fig. 9.9 Daily trading report

BAD DEBTS

These are normally presented as a percentage of turnover.
Included as bad debts would be forged travellers cheques, as well
as the usual non-payment of ledger accounts and 'walk-outs'.

METHOD OF PAYMENT

The frequency of the various payment methods can be recorded.
The breakdown can be useful in forecasting cash requirements and
in preparing cost and sales budgets. Allied to this is the calculation
of the length of debt on the sales ledger.

BUDGETS

Sales and cost budgets are normally prepared by management
from information that is gathered individually from each department of the hotel.

154

This system allocates income and expenditure into groups so that profit from each department can be more accurately calculated. Additionally, different hotels who use the system can then compare their operating ratios against each other and against any figures that are published nationally, because every unit that uses the system is calculating its figures and presenting them on the same basis.

Self-assessment questions

1 List three methods of calculating occupancy.
2 Show how any one of them is calculated.
3 Explain how the two methods of presenting average guest stay differ.
4 To what use can nationality statistics be put?
5 Draw a specimen housekeeper's report and explain its purpose.
6 What is meant by lead time?
7 What information is in a daily trading report?

Chapter 10
SOURCES OF BUSINESS

Chapter objectives

After studying this chapter you should be able to:
- identify the characteristics of the major sources of business for hotel accommodation;
- show how their different needs can be met by the front office.

It is important to the success of a hotel for the receptionist to be aware that not all guests are exactly the same, and that their needs may vary. This is the case with individuals, but there are some general characteristics which may be associated with the type of customer, whether they are from the UK or from overseas; whether they are booked by a travel agent, or a business house. This segmentation of the customers is the first step in preparing a sales plan for the front office of a hotel.

Agents

TRAVEL AGENTS

Travel agents are as varied in type and size as are hotels. There is the small agent who operates only one local office, but there are also the large international agents such as Thomas Cook and American Express who place millions of bookings a year for all types of business from offices in many different towns and countries.

The travel agent will make the booking for the guest and send a confirmation to the hotel. This booking may be only part of a whole series of hotel reservations and travel arrangements that the agent has made for a guest.

Confirmation of the booking is made on a confirmation form which has three copies. One is given to the guest, one sent to the hotel and the third is held by the agent. The travel agent will use this copy of the confirmation to claim commission from the hotel. The commission is a fixed percentage (10 per cent) of the accom-

```
┌─────────────────────────────────────────────────────────────┐
│                                                             │
│  EMPIRE TRAVEL                                              │
│  Bath Road                                                  │
│  GLOUCESTER                         Voucher No. 123456      │
│                                                             │
│  Hotel    Sea View          Address  Park Lane,            │
│                                      London, W.1.          │
│                                                             │
│  Accommodation   Double with Bath                          │
│                                                             │
│  Commencing with  Dinner         On       23/06/88         │
│                                                             │
│  Terminating with  Breakfast     On       26/06/87         │
│                                                             │
│  Including        Half Board                               │
│                                                             │
│  Client name      Mr & Mrs. H. Jauffret                    │
│                                                             │
│  Initials/Ref:    SEJ              Client (top) copy       │
│                                                             │
└─────────────────────────────────────────────────────────────┘
```

Fig. 10.1 Travel agent's voucher

modation rate before tax is added. Thus if a guest is booked for three nights in a room at £60 per night, the agent will claim commission of £18 for placing the booking with the hotel.

The agent may take prepayment from the guest, and issue him with a voucher which he can use at the hotel (*see* Fig. 10.1). Again, there are 3 copies of the voucher. On arrival at the hotel the guest gives the voucher to the receptionist and the amount of the voucher is allowed against the bill of the guest. At the end of the month the hotel will send all the vouchers from each agent back to the agency and the travel agent will pay the total amount owing minus the commission due.

HOTEL BOOKING AGENTS

A specialised form of agent is one that deals only with hotel reservations. The guest contacts the hotel booking agent who makes the reservation with the hotel and sends the confirmation both to the hotel and the guest. Hotel booking agents often have offices at major rail and air terminals and handle bookings for incoming passengers who do not have hotel reservations.

Commission is also collected from the hotel, but some agents only take commission on the first night booking, whilst others will claim on the full stay. Bookings which are made by hotel booking agents often have a higher non-arrival rate than normal bookings. Guests who arrive at a booking desk at an airport or railway station may make a booking with a hotel booking agent in case they cannot find an alternative. During the day, they will look around the town and attempt to find a hotel that is more suitable to their needs. If they do obtain alternative accommodation, then only a few will bother to contact the hotel and cancel their booking.

To minimise the problems caused by this, many hotels place all bookings by hotel booking agents on 6 pm release unless prepayment is made.

ALLOCATION/ALLOTMENT

Hotel booking agents and some business houses may negotiate an allocation of rooms at a particular hotel or with a group of hotels. This gives them a guaranteed number of rooms throughout the year; in this way, they can accommodate their regular customers even in periods of high demand. A hotel of 100 rooms may allocate 20 rooms to hotel booking agents and others. This allocation is normally placed on an 'automatic release' basis. If the agent has not made bookings for the rooms by a given date, then they are automatically reclaimed by the hotel. So, if five rooms are allocated to an agent on a seven-day release, and reservations have been made for only three of the rooms one week before the arrival date, the two remaining rooms are automatically released so that the hotel can sell them to ordinary customers. Rooms that are on allocation to an agent are charged at the same rate and in the same way as any other booking.

The allotment of rooms to an agent is beneficial to both parties. The hotel will gain by ensuring that the agent uses the hotel all year round. The agent saves time, for he does not have to contact the hotel to check if space is available, but can sell a room and simply send the confirmation to the hotel. Reception managers often extend the offer of an allocation of rooms to large companies that are regular users of the hotel. Again this is sound commercial sense, for it enables the company to obtain rooms even when the demand for accommodation is very high.

Other booking methods

AIRLINES

Airlines have expanded the services they offer passengers to include booking hotel accommodation. This service is free to airline passengers, but the airline will normally charge the hotel commission for acting as a booking agent.

Airline reservations are probably subject to the highest non-arrival rate of all bookings, for passengers change their plans, or perhaps the flight is delayed and the airline fails to notify the hotel. Bookings made by an airline are always placed on a release for the hotel has no knowledge of the identity of passengers other than their names; consequently it would be impossible to charge for non-arrival as the airline making the booking would not accept responsibility.

This is unlike a normal reservation where the guest, or the company, makes a booking directly with the hotel, so it is possible to locate the guest and request payment for non-arrival.

Some airlines have taken their links with hotels even further either by buying hotels, or developing their own hotel chains.

CONFERENCE BUSINESS

This is a valuable source of revenue to a hotel, especially if the conference takes place at a time when occupancy would otherwise be low. Discount rates are usually offered, or an all-in-one price for the conference rooms, the delegates' bedrooms and the food. Some hotels encourage partners to accompany the conference delegate by offering special rates known as two-for-one.

BUSINESS HOUSES

For many hotels, companies are their major source of business. Business people visiting regional offices or travelling around the country on sales trips are probably the largest source of demand for hotel accommodation in the UK. This demand exists all the year round, with the exception of public holidays. The company will often require accommodation at short notice and for this reason they prefer to establish close relations with hotels that they use on a regular basis.

An allocation of rooms to major business house users is one way of ensuring that a room is available at short notice. This allocation can be placed on a release as short as 24 hours.

Many companies will open ledger accounts with hotels and so speed the departure of guests at the end of their stay. Often customers' expenditure is higher with ledger accounts, for the guests are not constantly worrying whether they have enough money to settle their account on departure.

INDIVIDUALS

Guests who make their own reservations and pay their own bills upon departure are now rare for many city centre hotels. Some older hotels, though, specialise in this type of business.

Reservations are often made by letter, and the guests expect the personal attention to their requirements traditional in the hotel business.

Many holiday bookings fall into this category of individual bookings. With these bookings the reception department must always ensure that a confirmation is sent to the guest so that a correct address is verified before arrival. Also, notification of cheque limits and clearance times should be clearly brought to the attention of the guests. It is likely that guests who book to stay in a hotel on their own account are less frequent users of hotels and consequently less familiar with the systems and conventions that more seasoned travellers take for granted.

TOURISTS

For tourists the reception department is particularly important. Guests who are using the hotel as a base for a holiday will require from the reception assistance and advice on things to do and places to visit, together with information on how to travel there.

If the tourist is travelling individually, the receptionist can use local knowledge to increase the stay of the guest, by suggesting places that should be visited before the guest leaves the area.

Reservations from tourists have a long lead time, and if they are from overseas they may well be accompanied by a deposit to guarantee the arrival of the individual guest.

The expenditure from tourists, though, is often lower than for other guests of the hotel. One of the objectives of the trip may well be to enjoy as much variety as possible in food, and choice of restaurants. Consequently, the tourist may use the hotel restaurant far less.

TOUR OPERATORS

Some tourists prefer the security of an itinerary which has been planned on their behalf. These people will usually book through a tour operator at an all inclusive rate and travel with others from the same group. The hotel will base the rates it will offer on a variety of factors (*see* Chapter 8).

CENTRAL BOOKING OFFICES AND REFERRALS

A growing segment of business involves those guests who make the reservation through a company central reservation office, or who are referred to the hotel by another one in a chain or marketing group.

The guest may be either an individual travelling on business or a tourist.

Lead times of central booking office reservations tend to be shorter than many other forms of reservation. Unless the reservation is clearly made by a company, central booking office reservations are often treated as chance bookings and checks on credit status are carried out when the guest arrives at the hotel.

Referral reservations are made from one hotel to another in a group. They are widely used by tourists travelling by car; the lead for this form of business often comes from brochures displayed at the reception desk of the hotel. This is also done by hotels that are independent but members of marketing groups, such as Prestige Hotels or Best Western.

OTHER SEGMENTS

These are the major sources of business. Each of these can be further split into nationality of the guest, and even (for UK guests) which region of the country they come from. Again, the greater knowledge of the individual market segments of the hotel will enable the receptionists and front office staff to satisfy most effectively the wants and needs of these individuals and groups.

Self-assessment questions

1 Complete a specimen travel agent's voucher.
2 Explain the function of an allocation.
3 Why do hotel booking agents have more non-arrivals than other segments?
4 What are the benefits of business house customers?
5 What is the task of a central booking office?

Chapter 11
SELLING TECHNIQUES

Chapter objectives

After studying this chapter you should be able to:
- define the main market segments;
- state the purpose of selling;
- explain break-even point;
- define the main factors which influence customer choice;
- list the main methods of selling.

Reception as a sales department

The sales function has recently become an important and vital part of front office work. With more and more companies entering the Hotel and Catering field the public have had a much wider choice, and so it is essential for an establishment to present an attractive and economical product.

The consumer must be persuaded to buy the product and this factor of front office work has influenced the training and selection of reception staff. The receptionist must be capable of making a sale, since front office efficiency is judged on selling success. Sales techniques can be learned, although without doubt some people will have more of a flair for the work.

Although the marketing strategy will usually be devised by senior personnel it is the reception staff who will implement it, and so it is important that front office staff should be aware of the main objectives of marketing a hotel.

IDENTIFYING THE MARKET

Prior to attempting to sell a product it is important to identify the market. This can be done in a number of ways (*see* Chapter 9) but many organisations have a section on the registration/reservation card which will assist the management to identify the sector of the market to which the majority of customers belong.

Hotels frequently have a mixed market which is drawn from both business and holiday makers and each of the market segments may contribute an important part towards the revenue of the hotel.

The most frequently defined market segments are as follows:

1 conference
2 business house
3 independent traveller
4 local travellers
5 overseas holidays
6 domestic travellers

IDENTIFYING CUSTOMER NEEDS

Once the market has been established it is then necessary to indentify the needs of individual customers. Obviously those clients who are staying in the hotel for business purposes, probably segments 1–4, will be interested in the service which the hotel provides, may make frequent use of the telephone system, may require the use of a telex or fax machine, or may wish to entertain clients, either in the restaurant or in a suite. Tourists, on the other hand, may be far more concerned with friendly and willing service, since they may be on a limited budget, and use the additional hotel services less frequently.

MARKETING MIX

It is not impossible for a hotel to capture several sections of the market. It has already been shown that the price offered to a Tour Operator (see Chapter 8) may well have been reduced if the agent is placing a lot of business in the hands of the hotel.

Some establishments are particularly suited to large groups and tours, and find that by letting multiple occupancy rooms they are able to produce a product which fills a particular market. Other hotels may be eager to take their share of the tourist market, but are aware that tours and groups may not fit their image. In a case such as this a special promotion may be offered (e.g. golfing holidays), or a special rate which only applies at weekends.

Whatever strategy a hotel adopts it is essential to get the right business mix. A hotel which habitually accepts private clients would be very unwise to take a group of low paying tourists for the same period. Not only do many people feel unsettled by large groups it is also unwise to have clients paying full rack rate when others are staying at a substantial discount. Nonetheless the hotel is intent upon maximum occupancy and tourist business often provides a welcome source of revenue when the business clients go home for the weekend.

Purpose of selling

Obviously the hotel wants to make a profit every night, but it must also look towards the future, when it will also wish to make a profit. The sales function should really aim to satisfy two basic criteria:

1 Maximise the revenue to ensure the best profit.
2 Acheive customer satisfaction.

MAXIMISE REVENUE

Rooms can never be sold twice.

The first stage of understanding why sales are important in reception is that hotel rooms, as a saleable commodity, are strictly limited by factors of time and quantity. When selling accommodation hotels are selling one thing that has two separate parts. Accommodation consists of the room itself and a time factor. The customer buys room 210 on 23rd June. Room 210 on 24th June is a totally different commodity as far as sales are concerned. This makes hotel rooms similar to theatre or airline seats, where a time element is also involved, in that tickets are sold for the same seats on different days. Fig. 11.1 shows that if the room is not sold on the particular night concerned, then the revenue is lost for ever. This characteristic is unlike those of other commodities such as drinks or meals, where the product can be stored until it is requested by the customer. Therefore for many goods availability (or production) is more important than selling, but for hotel rooms the reverse is true. Selling is the task of paramount importance because the number of rooms available cannot be affected in the short term to match demand.

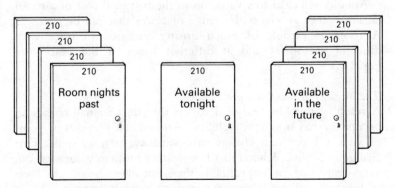

Fig. 11.1 Relationship between room and time

How much profit is there in a room sale?
Economists talk of marginal cost as the cost of producing one
more unit of production. In a hotel the unit of production is a
room. The marginal cost of a hotel room (*see* Fig. 11.2) is the cost
of the items that are used by the guest whilst staying. Not
included are those things that would have to be provided or paid
for whether or not the room is sold.

Marginal cost items	Not included
Registration card	Wages of receptionist and maid
Guest bill	
Electricity in guest room	Electricity in public areas
Water heating for bath	
	T.V. Licence and telephone rental
Laundry of linen	
Soap	Rent and rates

Fig. 11.2 Marginal cost of a guest room

Even in a top class London hotel the marginal cost of the room
is unlikely to exceed £5.50. The difference between the marginal
cost and the selling price is the contribution towards fixed costs
and profits.

For a restaurant the marginal cost of a meal or a drink will be
a much greater proportion of the selling price. Often the food cost
of a meal is 40 per cent of the selling price.

Each extra room sale will provide a greater contribution to
profits than each extra meal sale.

Another effect of this variation in the marginal cost of a room
(against other goods) is the range of prices that can be charged.
A room is capable of much greater variation in price with
different customers and at different times of the year. (*See*
Fig. 11.3.)

The break-even point and profitability
A result of this low marginal cost is the effect a small change in
occupancy has upon profitability. Around the break-even point
of sales a 1 per cent change in occupancy means a 3 per cent
change in profits. A hotel that is operating profitably one year can
very easily become unprofitable the next, even though the level
of business will only have dropped by a small amount. This is

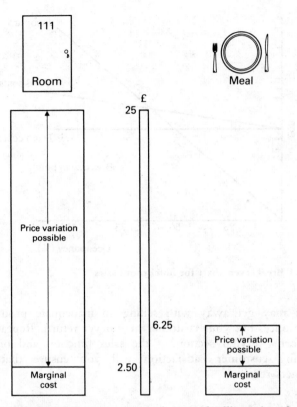

Fig. 11.3 Relationship between marginal cost and selling price of room and meal

clearly shown in Fig. 11.4 which also highlights the high fixed costs of operating a hotel.

In Fig. 11.4 break–even (the point at which the hotel is covering all of its costs, but not making a profit) is at 65 per cent occupancy.

This rather lengthy explanation of the economics of operating a hotel shows clearly that sales are the most important feature of running a hotel profitably. A manager who spends his or her time on buying, to cut the marginal costs of selling rooms, is not using time effectively, for there is a much greater return in increasing sales, and this should be the area of greatest effort.

ACHIEVING CUSTOMER SATISFACTION

There is an old saying about pleasing some of the people some of time, some of the people all of the time, but never all of the people all of the time. Selling is a bit like this.

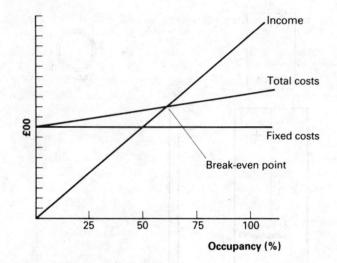

Fig. 11.4 Break-even chart for hotel room sales

You may get away with selling an inadequate product or service once, but your customer may never return. Repeat business forms a vital section of the sales function and only by achieving customer satisfaction will you ensure that your customers return.

The hotel product

Selling the facilities to the guest is unique in the opportunity it offers. If the guest is away from home, then it is almost certain that they will want to have a meal and a drink during their stay: intelligent selling by the receptionist will ensure that the hotel's restaurant facilities are promoted fully. A guest who has been travelling for a few days will be delighted to hear of the laundry and dry cleaning service which the hotel offers. The job of the receptionist is to find out the needs of individual guests and suggest ways of satisfying them.

The hotel product could be divided into four main areas:

1 accommodation
2 food
3 drink
4 services.

Selling by reception employees involves finding the needs of customers, converting them into wants, and providing the facilities to fulfil them.

CUSTOMER CHOICE

There are several basic reasons why a customer may choose a particular product, and the hotel product is no different to any other.

Need

A customer may buy a hotel room, even if it is not what is really wanted, simply because they need the product. The traveller who is already tired and has driven a long way may feel they need a room so badly that they would pay rather more than usual, or accept something below their normal standards.

Security

Many customers, even those who travel frequently, need the security of staying in familiar surroundings. Hotels which promote a group image provide guests with this type of security, since they can be sure of familiar surroundings whatever country they are staying in.

Comfort

A client may be influenced by comfortable surroundings and subsequently buy the product on view. This is why many hotels take great care to ensure that their front hall facilities are inviting and comfortable, and that their restaurant and bar will immediately put customers at their ease.

Desire

This is one of the most common reasons for making a purchase, the customer sees the product and wants it. Many sales are made through impulse buying and for hotels in particular a brochure can influence a potential customer so that they really want to stay in that particular hotel.

Pride

Some customers will purchase a product because they want to be seen owning it. This is particularly true of items like cars where people will pay a great deal of money for a product to be proud of. The same can often be true of hotels—some customers will only stay in an establishment that they can be proud to come back to.

Pleasure

This is one of the best reasons for making a purchase—because it gives you pleasure. Customers of this type are usually very easy to please because they are intent upon enjoying themselves. In a hotel particularly it is important to ensure that your customers' pleasure in not spoiled, and they will continue to stay with you because they enjoy it.

Fear

A strange reason for buying a product but a common one. People buy an umbrella because they are afraid it might rain. Customers buy hotel rooms occasionally even though it is really not what they want.

A customer may find a room too expensive or not at all to their taste. If it is 23.00 hours and everywhere is full the client may well accept the room because they are afraid they will get nothing else.

Fashion

Fashion plays a big part in high street sales, but also makes a contribution to hotel sales. Hotels and restaurants can be 'fashionable' according to who goes there, or the write up they receive in the press and hotel guides. Many customers want to be seen at the latest 'in' place.

Habit

Many clients will buy the product because they always do. This does not mean that a hotel can afford to be complacent, they must ensure that their standard remains as good as ever, then the customer will continue with the habit. These are just some of the basic reasons why a customer will purchase a product. If there is plenty of availability and the customer is free to make a choice there are other crieteria which influence selection.

Location

One of the most important reasons for staying in a hotel is its location. Customers arriving late at night after a long flight will often choose an airport hotel because of its convenient location, even though the city centre may be only fifteen miles away.

In order to boost sales a receptionist must be aware of the exact location of the hotel, its access by road and rail, and any other information which may help a prospective client. It is also essential to know the name of the nearest large town if applicable and any local places of interest.

Facilities
Obviously a customer will be influenced to make a choice according to the facilities which are on offer at a hotel.

Some clients require little more than cleanliness and pleasant service, while others will require 24 hour service in all departments. The receptionist must know all the facilities which the hotel offers and the prices if appropriate. The availability of car parking and garage facilities are often of concern to a propestive guest and the front office staff should ensure they are familiar with all sections of the hotel.

Checklists should be compiled for all the other sales outlets and facilities of the hotel. In a large hotel, these are likely to include banqueting, meeting rooms, florist, swimming pool, car hire, sauna, hairdresser, theatre tickets, laundry/valet, kiosk shop, sports facilities.

With so many facilities and sales outlets, only the most skilled receptionist will know details of all of them without referring to a product fact sheet, but every receptionist should know to whom queries should be referred. This is especially necessary for sales leads that may come in for banqueting and conferences.

Value for money
Even the most wealthy of clients still want to see value for money. Most people have no objection to paying for a service, even a fairly expensive one, but they do not like to feel that they have been cheated. If some of your rooms are more expensive than others explain why. You do not have to be apologetic about price increases, merely ensure that the client is aware of the increase in benefits and services.

Selling methods

A receptionist must be aware of the different skills and techniques required when selling.
In general terms sales can be made in several different ways:

1 personal
2 telephone
3 correspondence
4 telex.

Whichever method is in use many of the basic techniques remain the same. Of all the methods available face to face selling opens up the most opportunity for front office staff to demonstrate their skill.

PERSONAL SELLING

Selling face to face is a key task for the receptionist. This means actively promoting the facilities of the hotel rather than being passive and merely responding to guests' queries and requests. A personal sales campaign can increase sales of a hotel dramatically, even if it is already trading at a high occupancy.

USP

The first step in personal selling is for the receptionist to develop a unique sales proposition (USP) for the hotel. This is something that occurs only in that particular unit. The product analysis will provide some useful leads which can be compared against the competition in the area. Typical USPs may be:

(*a*) we have a covered garage;
(*b*) our night porter will serve food at any time;
(*c*) our pool contains fresh water;
(*d*) the restaurant is in the *Good Food Guide*;
(*e*) all our telephones are direct dial;
(*f*) there is no extra charge for children under the age of twelve.

These USPs should be introduced as a benefit in sales presentation by the receptionist.

DESCRIPTIVE WORDS

When selling to a potential customer, front office staff should be encouraged to use descriptive words wherever possible. Some attribute of the room should always be mentioned; 'a centrally heated room', 'a twin room with a view of the park', or 'including television with bedside controls'. All of these things expand the benefits for the guests and help them visualise the room. This use of description must always be followed when talking about the price of a room. A question on price should always be answered with a full explanation of the facilities that the price includes; the price of a room should never be mentioned alone.

OFFER ALTERNATIVES

Professional sales staff always offer alternatives to a prospective customer. To avoid confusion, these should always be limited to two. If a guest requests a double room, the receptionist should reply, 'We can let you have 210, with a private bath, for £60 per night, or 305, which is larger and has a view of the park, for £85' The guest now has a simple choice between 210 and 305, and is aware of the extra benefits of the more expensive room. If in response to the request the receptionist simply offered 210 at £60 per night, the guest is left to choose between taking it or leaving it. They may well not take the room; even if they did take it, the £25 extra revenue from 305 may be lost.

ABC OF SELLING

A simple way of classifying selling by the hotel receptionist is the approach of 'ABC'. This classifies sales into three groups:

A—automatic;
B—bettered;
C—created.

Automatic sales

These are the most common in any hotel. The receptionist is merely acting as an order taker. The customer knows clearly what is required; all the receptionist does is take the details and fill out the reservation form. Many receptionists never progress beyond this first level of selling.

Bettered sales

These are generally described as 'selling up' which is an important method of increasing average rates in hotels. A bettered sale is 'more of the same'. It is a suite instead of a double room, a room with a private bath instead of a room with a shower. Opportunities for a bettered sale may come by intelligent questioning of the guest, or observation, as he or she is checking in. A guest who wishes to stay for a week may take a slightly more expensive room if they are told that it has more wardrobe space. A guest who arrives in an expensive car, but has only booked a single room, may react favourably to the offer of a two-room suite. A skilful receptionist will fit the sale to the prospective guest and learn to identify customers who would appreciate the offer of superior or larger accommodation.

Even the guest who has booked a single room can be told 'Mr Green, since you made your reservation a room with a large bed has become vacant; it is larger and on the side of the hotel that faces the park. Would you prefer that to the room we are holding for you?'

Created sale

The created sale is the sale that the guest did not request, but will accept gratefully. Created sales involve real selling. A created sale is another product entirely. In hotels, created sales would include

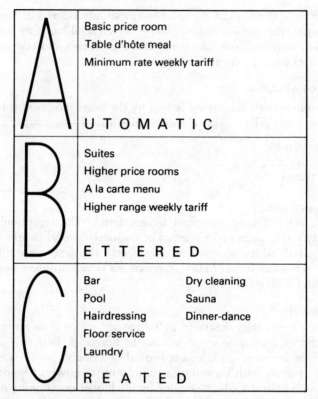

Fig. 11.5 ABC of hotel sales

floor service, dry cleaning, hairdressing, restaurant facilities, sauna—the list is endless. Creative selling in a hotel is relatively easy, for the guest is certain to want to eat. All the receptionist has to do is to show the guest the opportunities that are available. This form of selling must also be fitted to the customer. If a guest checks in at 11 a.m., they should be offered morning coffee, or a booking for lunch in the restaurant. A guest who checks in at 4 p.m. may want to have some clothes pressed before going out to a dinner-dance. A guest who arrives late at night can be offered sandwiches and a drink from floor service. A receptionist may be shy of being 'pushy'; creative selling, however, entails rather satisfying guests' needs and increasing the average expenditure at the hotel. The split of hotel facilities into 'A', 'B' and 'C' class sales is shown in Fig. 11.5

RETURN VISITS

The easiest person to sell to is an existing customer. They know and use the hotel already. Getting a guest to book a return visit is a key part of reception selling. As a guest checks out they should be asked if they are returning again in the future. If the answer is 'yes', then the receptionist can offer to reserve space for them. Many receptionists treat the task of booking return visits as an obstacle race with the guest as the obstacle! Remarks such as 'We are very full then but I will see what I can do' are not designed to make a departing guest feel wanted. Return guests are the lifeblood of a successful hotel and should be encouraged whenever possible.

TELEPHONE SALES

Most sales made by telephone in a hotel are from incoming sales. This is the most effort-free form of sales, since the mere fact that the client has called your hotel rather than any other means a choice has already been made. The receptionist should ensure that the client's interest is held, and subsequently converted to a sale.

Basic telephone techniques should be observed to make sure the client receives a good impression of the efficiency of the hotel (*see* Chapter 4) and the front office staff should ensure that they are well equipped with a product fact sheet so that all enquiries can be answered.

SELLING BY LETTER/TELEX

Sales letters
Circular letters are often useful in generating sales leads for the hotel and its facilities. Reception staff should be aware that a campaign is going on, and be fully knowledgeable of the terms if offers. They will then be able to pass on enquiries to the correct member of management.

A sales letter should follow the traditional salesman's 'AIDA' model in order to be effective. This means that the letter should be arranged in the following way:

A attention
The beginning of the letter should be designed to gain the attention of the recipient. Not the normal 'Dear Sir, I am writing on behalf of the Grand Hotel to inform you . . .' but something that will make the reader want to carry on such as 'In this letter there are three ways you can increase your company profits. . . .'

Fig. 11.6 Telephone sales

I interest
The body of the letter should capture the interest of the reader. This is best done by always presenting the material in the form of client benefits. Any letter that carries 'I' or 'we' or 'our' is wrong. It should be 'you' and 'your'.

D desire
Desire is the next stage of this mnemonic; the customer should

be encouraged to find out more, to see the new facilities, to use the bargain break, and so on.

A action
The final part is action. This converts the interest and desire into a booking or enquiry. Again, it should not be 'If I can help you in any way, please telephone my secretary for an appointment'. Some companies issue a challenge to stimulate action on the part of the potential customer. A very successful sales campaign was based on the challenge, 'If we do not answer the phone before five rings, then hang up and call the opposition.'

Regardless of the medium which is used most sales begin with an initial enquiry, or a tentative offer. This is your opportunity to open the sale. You may begin by offering a room for the period in question, and quoting the price. If handled correctly the client's interest will be retained and you may then go on to develop the sale. This gives you the chance to describe the room and its facilities, and stress the value of the room for the price. You may decide at this point to show the customer the room if they are hesitant, and take the opportunity to point out all the good points of the hotel as you go.

Once the guest is sold on the product it is time for your to close the sale. Get a commitment, or even better, a deposit or prepayment.

HANDLING OBJECTIONS

Every experienced receptionist will be aware of the objections that are used when an attempt is made to sell something to a guest; 'It is too expensive' is probably the most common response. A fully trained receptionist will not be put off by an objection, instead they will have developed individual strategies to overcome the most common objections in their unit. It is only an amateur who is put off by the first objection that a prospective guest raises; the skilled receptionist will handle the objection and still try and sell the facilities of the hotel to the customer.

Self assessment questions

1 What are the main market segments in a hotel?
2 Why can a hotel room never be sold twice?
3 What makes up the marginal cost of a hotel room?
4 What areas in the hotel product divided into?
5 List the main reasons why a customer chooses a particular product.
6 Describe the main selling methods in use in hotels.

Chapter 12

SELLING AND THE FRONT OFFICE

Chapter objectives

After studying this chapter you should be able to:
- show the need for the sales effort in hotel front offices;
- Outline ways in which repeat business can be sought;
- identify product analysis;
- state the main aids to sales.

The need for sales

Selling has been recognised as part of the work of a receptionist for many years, but most sales training has concentrated upon the 'public relations' aspect of the work. It is only recently that some hotels have systematically trained their reception staff to increase sales of the whole hotel, and also the company they work for.

In order that selling from the reception desk is effective it must have the active support of top management. This is essential for a number of reasons. Reception staff will be positive towards sales if they see management acting in the same way. If a member of management attempts to increase sales in dealing with guests, then the staff will follow the example. Sometimes through emphasising sales and achieving 100 per cent occupancy, the front office staff will be working under great pressure, especially if it is necessary to book out guests. At this time it is essential that members of management are available to handle the guests booked out and support the reception staff. Finally management support is needed to ensure that there is no friction between departments. If reception staff are taking orders for the restaurant or floor service, it is important that these orders are dealt with promptly and courteously.

Without active management participation, any plan for the reception to increase sales systematically will be a failure.

Front office staff should be aware of the sales leads which form an important part of the marketing of the hotel.

Mail shots and other information will make much more impact if they are assured to reach the right person.

Sales leads can often be obtained from the following sources:

CORRESPONDENCE AND ENQUIRIES

These, when checked, can often constitute an invaluable contribution to sales. Correspondence will often reveal why a client is staying in the hotel, and whether they intend to return. It may be prudent to send details of new developments, or information regarding other special tariffs such as 2 for 1 or Christmas programmes.

Every enquiry should be followed up, and where specific questions have been asked, a sale is more likely to be made if a personal reply is received by the prospective client.

REPEAT CUSTOM

Every client who enters the hotel is potentially a repeat source of business. This is particularly true of customers who attended special weekends, since they may well be interested in other similar functions which the hotel is organising.

LOCAL PAPER

This is an important source of information regarding forthcoming events in the locality. Many young people announce their engagement and so make an ideal selling lead to a wedding reception.

Local companies may also be approached for Christmas parties, or invited to 'open' days to view your facilities.

UNUSUAL BOOKING PATTERNS

Most hotels have a definite pattern and can expect to predict their occupancy well in advance. If an unusual pattern emerges (e.g. you are full well in advance at a weekend when you are usually quite empty) it would be prudent to find out why this is so. The increase in booking may be attributable to a national event, in which case great care should be taken to ensure that letting is being carried out sensibly, or it may be due to a local company's function. In this case it would be wise to find out if they often hold functions of this type, or to check to see if they are making full use of the facilities in the hotel.

REFERRALS

Referral bookings are an important source of revenue to any hotel, and should be followed up as a potential sales lead. A consortium who produce a group brochure may find that it is worthwhile circulating the information to all clients in the hope that they may utilise the other hotels in the group, or recommend them to friends.

The hotel product

The first stage of increasing sales in a hotel is a full knowledge of the facilities the hotel offers, the way they can be offered for sale, and the terms of business. Tariffs, package tours and restaurant promotions all go to make up the 'product' that the receptionist is selling. A hotel is in this respect no different to any other product that is offered for sale. Certainly, it is larger and more complex than many items that are sold in shops, but the fundamental skills of selling still apply.

Hotel name _____

Address _____

Telephone _____ Telex _____ Cable _____

Owned by _____ General manager _____

Rooms   **Rate**

  Singles _____ _____ Check-in

  Twins _____ _____

  Doubles _____ _____ Check-out

  Suites _____ _____

Transport connections

Road   Nearest parking

Bus

Rail

Star rating   A.A. _____ R.A.C. _____

Listed in guide books   1 _____

                               2 _____

                               3 _____

Restrictions _____

Fig. 12.1 Product fact sheet

PRODUCT ANALYSIS

This technique provides a clear knowledge of exactly what constitutes the product. For a hotel this may be more complex than it first seems. The hotel building itself is the first part of the product analysis. The receptionist should know the location and full address including the postcode, the telephone, telex number and the telemessage address. Linked with this, the receptionist should be able to explain clearly to the guest how to reach the hotel by all forms of public and private transport. For private transport, the receptionist should know parking facilities and any restrictions or charges that apply. The total number of rooms and their variety, and the star rating together with details of the ownership of the hotel may be requested of a receptionist. This information is often kept on a product fact sheet in the reception area (*see* Fig. 12.1).

PEOPLE

Members of the management are an important part of the hotel 'product' so all the receptionists should be able to recognise and know the names of all members of the management in the hotel. A potential guest who asks for Mr Evans and is told that he is not resident will not have a great deal of faith in the hotel if Mr Evans is the name of the banqueting manager.

A common practice in many large hotels is to display photographs of key management personnel in reception. This way reception staff will become familiar not only with the names of senior staff, but also learn to recognise them by sight.

ROOMS

For the receptionist the individual guest rooms are the most important part of the hotel. It is not possible to sell a room to a potential guest with only partial knowledge of the benefits. Fig. 12.2 is a checklist for each room in the hotel.

All of these points may be stored in a room inventory card at the front desk. A simple way of classifying rooms in a larger hotel that is not a new property is to have a ranking system. The best rooms in each type are Class 1 rooms, the next best Class 2 and so on. By doing this, the receptionist will be able to sell rooms selectively, emphasising the particular benefits of each one. Naturally this is facilitated by the use of a computer in the reservations department, although in many large modern hotels, where all rooms tend to be exactly the same, it is not so necessary. Some American hotels have adopted the technique of storing photo-

```
Exact location in hotel _____

Number of beds and size_____

Furniture and fittings _____

Bathroom/shower/toilet?_____

Power points, location and rating _____

Furnishings and style _____

Telephone, radio, television? _____

Heating and air conditioning? _____

View from window _____

Noise levels _____

Access for handicapped? _____

Nearest lift _____
```

Fig. 12.2 Checklist for individual guest room

graphs of typical rooms at the front desk so that a client may see a room before making a decision. On the Continent it is common practice for the guest to be taken to see the room before actually buying and this is a procedure rapidly being adopted by many hotels in the UK.

The basis of room product analysis is to assist the receptionist in selling the room to potential guests. To familiarise receptionists with rooms some hotels encourage the staff to sleep in a vacant room when they are on late/early shift. This is a very effective way of building up a new receptionist's product knowledge. Another idea is to ensure that each new receptionist spends a period of time with a floor housekeeper. This not only aids internal 'geography' but may help both staff members to be more sympathetic to each other's problems.

PUBLIC AREAS

Lounges, reading rooms, toilets and other public areas in the hotel should be known to the receptionist. Then they will be able to direct guests throughout the hotel and recommend the most appropriate place for a guest to sit quietly, or wait for a friend.

FOOD AND BEVERAGE FACILITIES

These are second only to the guest rooms in importance to a guest. The receptionist should know full details of every food and beverage outlet in the hotel. Many hotels assist the receptionist by displaying a copy of the menu and bar tariff at the front desk, so that they can be shown to guests who enquire about the facilities. Fig. 12.3 shows a product checklist for all food and beverage outlets. This should be carried out in every bar and restaurant and also for floor service and the lounge.

Only if the receptionist is fully knowledgeable of the food and beverage outlets will they be able to satisfy the individual needs as efficiently as possible.

Location in hotel _____	Decor/theme _____
Opening times _____	Special features _____
Last orders _____	Menu details _____
Licensed? _____	Charge to room? _____
Dress rules _____	Name of restaurant manager _____
Average expenditure _____	Booking necessary? _____
Minimum charge _____	
Credit cards _____	

Fig. 12.3 Product checklist for food and beverage facilities

RULES

An important part of product analysis is a clear knowledge of any rules and restrictions that may be in force in the establishment. Equally necessary is an understanding of why they operate, so that they can be explained intelligently to the guest. Obviously these will vary from one hotel to the next, but important ones will probably concern check out times, prepayment for chance bookings, payment by cheque, last orders in the restaurant, extensions of stay and so on.

COMPETITION

The last stage of product analysis concerns the facilities offered by other hotels and restaurants in the area. If a receptionist knows what the competition offers and what its strong points are then they will be able to meet the objections of the guest and emphasise the strong points of their own property.

Aids to sales

Most hotels now take advantage of the many 'giveaways' and printed material available to remind the guests of their stay in the hotel, but it is important to realise that in themselves these items do not constitute a selling aid. They will merely serve to remind the guest of the name and telephone number of the establishment, and hopefully of the enjoyable stay they passed there. Printed material of this nature includes:

pocket calendars
book matches
pens
key rings
telephone pads

BROCHURES

Descriptive brochures of the hotel should always be available at the front desk, and staff should be encouraged to give them to guests and casual enquirers. If the brochure has a picture of a room in it, then it can be a useful visual aid for the receptionist when selling rooms. Tariffs are normally printed separately as an insert, so that price changes do not make the brochures useless. If the hotel is in a chain or marketing consortium then the brochures of other group hotels should be kept in a display rack at the front desk.

DISPLAYS

An opportunity is often available for a hotel to 'display its goods' in the same way as a shop. This example of merchandising displays can be as simple as a refrigerated cabinet of food outside the coffee shop, or it could be a window display of the banqueting room set up for a conference. Every opportunity should be taken to catch the client's atteniton in this manner.

PRICE

For most clients the price is an important influence upon the final selection of a hotel, and for many years retailers have realised the importance of price as a sales aid. Clothing has always been sold for £9.99 and detergent products have a long history of being offered at 5p off.

It is only recently that the importance of price has been acknowledged by some hoteliers. Even today there are hotels and restaurants that offer goods for sale at a price plus VAT and a cover charge. The receptionist should be fully aware of the price of all the rooms in the hotel, what the price includes and what extra charges there are. As the market for accommodation becomes more sophisticated so price variations increase. Many London hotels have six separate rates for each room dependent upon the class of business and time of year. This is sensible business practice for it segments the market into different sections and charges them accordingly. Examples of these sections could be business people, tours, conventions, celebrities, long-stay guests, airline personnel and so on.

The actual tariff can also be used as a sales tool to attract guests at different times, and to different types of hotel. A brief explanation of the different tariffs is given below.

Room only (European plan)
This is a rate for the room, with no meals included. It is commonly used in luxury hotels in city centres.

Room and breakfast (Continental plan)
Breakfast may be either English or continental; some hotels include continental breakfast in the tariff and charge a supplement for English breakfast. Often a supplement is also charged if the breakfast is taken in the guest's room.

Half board (demi-pension, Modified American Plan)
This includes room, breakfast and one other meal. Hotels will vary in offering lunch, dinner or a choice of either for the meal. There is no set rule. Resort hotels use this tariff extensively because it increases the average guest expenditure, and ensures use of the hotel restaurant.

Full board (en pension, American Plan)
Again some resort hotels offer full board to the guests. It generally includes room, breakfast, lunch and dinner, although some hotels may also include afternoon tea in the rate.

All-inclusive terms
An extension of full board is the practice of some hotels. These

charge a daily rate and include in this all meals, and also unlimited use of the sports and social facilities of the hotel. This is a very attractive package for resort hotels, and makes accounting easier.

Two for one
Business hotels sometimes offer a rate where the spouse of a guest is given free accommodation. This promotional device is aimed at encouraging guests to bring their wives or husbands with them on business trips. The hotel hopes to benefit by increased use of food and beverage facilities. Often offers of this type are made in conjunction with airlines who give discounts on spouse fares.

Children free
Many hotels will accommodate children free of charge, or at a nominal rate if they share the same room as their parents.

The principle of tariff structures and price discounting is to tailor the product as closely as possible to the needs of the market. Price cutting alone is a very blunt tool, for it will probably only result in a lower total income. Also, a price cut can be easily and quickly matched by the competition. For certain segments of the market price cutting is not necessary; businessmen, for example, often do not pay their own accounts and so are not sensitive to the price charged. At the top end of the market, high prices may be a positive advantage; some people will make a point of only using the most expensive hotel in an area.

PACKAGE BUILDING

A technique being increasingly used to promote sales in hotels is the offer of a special 'package' deal. This is often promoted during the off season for weekend business.

With a package accommodation, meals and other facilities are put together and sold at an inclusive price. Marketing is carried out through posters, brochures and advertising, under a brand name, such as 'Mini Breaks', 'Weekend Breaks' or 'Bargain Breaks'. Not all constituents of the package need be provided in the hotel. Some recent imaginative packages have included theatre tickets, entrance fees to exhibitions, pocket cameras, T-shirts and visits to nearby places of interest.

The basis of a package is to make it easy for the prospective customer to buy, and to give them an incentive to come. By putting together a number of facilities and goods and selling at an inclusive 'no extras' price the product can be marketed as 'value for money', because price comparison is difficult.

Supporting the sales effort

The receptionist, although an important member of a hotel sales team, can only work effectively with the assistance of management. Successful sales campaigns are supported by the following material and actions.

MARKET RESEARCH

Systematic market research is an invaluable tool in increasing sales. The key is to make it systematic. The manager standing in the bar and talking to guests who seem approachable is a poor substitute for a planned market survey. It is quite easy to carry out desk research and find a customer profile. Many computer programs are designed to accumulate as much marketing information about a guest as possible, and this certainly facilitates research. Facts such as where guests come from, how long they stay and what they spend can all be gathered from registration cards or bills.

Registration cards additionally can ask for other useful information such as occupation, purpose of visit or why your particular hotel was chosen. Another method of carrying out research is to insert questionnaires in guest rooms. These are often used to assess standards of service and hotel facilities (*see* Fig. 12.4).

Guests may also be asked what extra facilities should be provided in the hotel. In this way the hotel is more likely to provide the facilities that are actually wanted by guests, rather than those that management think they want.

Many people think they will automatically get repeat business—this is not so. Guests are more and more demanding and the front office staff must be aware of all the various ways in which sales can be made. It is not enough for the receptionist to be polite, well turned out and personable, smiling pleasantly at all the guests. These are merely basic social skills and alone they will never result in a sale.

The front office staff must be taught sales techniques so that the customer will be aware of all the facilities of the hotel. As the guests are away from home and in an unfamiliar environment, they will need assistance in satisfying their everyday needs in strange surroundings; it is the prime task of the receptionist to provide this assistance.

We value your opinion!

Dear guest, could you fill out this
questionnaire to tell us how we are
succeeding in meeting the needs of
our guests — Thank you

Room no. _____   Date _____

Rooms	Good	Average	Poor
Clean	☐	☐	☐
Comfortable	☐	☐	☐
Maid service	☐	☐	☐
Restaurant			
Quality	☐	☐	☐
Service	☐	☐	☐
Price	☐	☐	☐
Reception			
Service	☐	☐	☐
Attitude	☐	☐	☐

Your comments _____

_____

_____

Signature _____

Fig. 12.4 Guest room questionnaire

TRAINING

Sales staff need to be trained. Only the most determined receptionist will attempt to increase sales without assistance. Sales training is often based upon films, lectures and role playing away from the reception desk. Here reception staff can try out the techniques of increasing business without the fear of getting it wrong in front of a guest. It is then only a small step to transfer it to the workplace, with the active support of the reception manager.

KNOWLEDGE OF RESULTS

Many people feel that this is the most important part of a sales campaign. Reception staff need to know how successful they are. Everyone wants to know how they are getting on. Management must give feedback to front office personnel on how a campaign is going. This is often linked with sales targets. A target may be to increase the average rate by 10 per cent. If regular information is posted on how near the target is to being met this can act as a very powerful motivator.

REWARDS

Feedback alone will probably not be sufficient. Management should introduce some system of reward for the extra effort by front office staff. This could be either group based, for all the staff on one shift, or individual rewards for each receptionist. The choice depends upon the particular sales campaign.

An occupancy bonus is one of the most common systems of rewarding reception staff. Every front office employee gains a bonus if a target occupancy is reached. Some companies operate a single, double and triple bonus scheme, paying £2, £4 and £6 above the normal weekly wage for different target occupancy levels. These levels are based on last year's occupancy. It is certainly worthwhile for the hotel to do this, for once past break-even point the increase in profit would far outweigh the cost of paying the bonus.

In addition to this some units give champagne to all reception staff every time 100 per cent occupancy is reached.

Commission is another technique used for some sales campaigns. Here receptionists are rewarded with a fixed amount for each sale of a specified product. 10p for each restaurant booking made by a receptionist is an example of a commission scheme. It must be well administered, however, or it may create rivalry between individual receptionists to the detriment of the comfort of the guests.

Another common incentive is to promote an 'employee of the month' campaign, offering valuable prizes to staff as a reward for effort. 'Receptionist of the month' is a title used by some companies who select the receptionist they feel has increased sales most during the preceding month. Prizes of weekend breaks, or dinner for two are often given in schemes of this kind.

Selling is an integral part of the work of the receptionist but it is likely to be the area given the least attention by management. However, a well planned front office sales effort is a very effective way of increasing profits and at the same time maximising the satisfaction of the individual guests of a hotel.

Self-assessment questions

1 List the main sales leads in hotels.
2 What are the major aids to sales?
3 Describe the principal hotel tariffs in use.
4 Why is training an important part of front office sales?
5 What information would be included in a Product Fact Sheet?

GLOSSARY OF TERMS

Accommodation and taxi order (A and TO). A voucher issued by airlines to cover the cost of travellers who are delayed whilst on a flight. It is redeemable by the airline at face value, and normally covers accommodation, breakfast, a main meal and return taxi fare from the airport to the hotel.

Advance booking chart The chart which is kept to inform the reservation staff of the level of bookings for any date in the future. The two main types are the conventional chart and the density chart.

Advise duration and charge (AD and C) Hotel telephone operators when using an exchange assisted call ask the exchange operator to inform the hotel of the time of the call and the cost, so that it can be charged onto the guest's account. This charge often has a surcharge placed on it to cover hotel costs.

Allowance A deduction made on a guest's bill, either through posting a charge to the wrong account, or possibly as a reduction for a disputed service, or complaint.

American plan see Full board

Arrival list An alphabetical list of all guests due to arrive on a given day. It is often cross referenced to the bookings diary.

Assistant manager The role of assistant manager will vary from one hotel to another. He may have line responsibility for a particular department, but in American owned hotels, is more likely to be a general 'customer relations' employee who liaises with guests.

Audit roll Located in the billing machine, the audit roll provides a printed record of every transaction carried out on the machine. Many machines are constructed so that they will only operate if the roll is in place.

Average rate This shows the average income per room. Generally calculated on a daily and monthly basis.

Back to back Tours and group bookings that arrive on the same day as the previous one is leaving are called 'back to back'. There is no gap in the accommodation taken, for the room is continuously occupied throughout the season.

Bed and breakfast Room and breakfast at an inclusive rate. The breakfast can be either English or Continental. It is left to the customer to ascertain exactly what he is purchasing.

Bedroom book The simplest form of room status system, showing who is occupying each room. It can also be used for reservations. Commonly found in smaller hotels.

Bed sheet Medium sized hotels use a bed sheet to show who is in each room. It is filled out each evening by the duty receptionist. Some forms have three columns showing arrivals, guests in house and departures.

Bill office A separate department of the front office where guests' accounts are prepared.

Block booking A reservation for a group of people travelling together, either on tour or company function.

Bonding Insurance taken out on people who handle large sums of cash; bonding is a protection against dishonest staff.

Brought forward The outstanding total of guests' accounts from the previous day's business.

Carried forward The outstanding total of guests' accounts that are taken into the next day's business.

Cashier's office A separate department in the front office that takes money from guests in payment of accounts and carries out foreign exchange transactions. It may also handle safe deposit of guests' valuables.

Central booking office (CBO) A reservation office that handles bookings for all the hotels in a group or marketing consortia.

'Chance' A guest who stays at a hotel without a previous reservation. This term can also be applied to restaurant guests.

Check-in Registration of guest.

Check-out Departure of guest.

Chef de brigade Reception shift leader.

Cheque card A card issued by banks to guarantee cheques up to a set amount.

City ledger see Sales ledger.

Close out A system to control reservations—staff are instructed not to accept bookings over certain busy periods. The chart will be 'closed out' for rooms of certain types on certain days.

Commercially important person (CIP) A client who has influence over a large amount of business.

Commission A payment made to an agent for introducing business.

Commissionaire see Doorman

Concierge see Head porter

Conference business A group of delegates using a meeting room in the hotel but ideally making use of other facilities such as accommodation, food and beverage.

Confirmation A letter or telex from a guest confirming details of a reservation.

Consortium A number of independently owned hotels who join together to gain the advantages of group ownership.

Continental breakfast A simple breakfast of beverage, bread and preserves.

Continental plan Room and continental breakfast.

Control Responsible for checking charges and postings made by departments.

Conventional chart A reservation chart that shows individual guest rooms.

Correction A charge made to a bill to adjust for a previous error.

Credit card A card which allows guests to charge their account for later payment to the card company.

Day let A room let out for use during the day, often for business meetings.

Deadline A date by which provisional bookings have to be confirmed.

Debtors ledger see Sales ledger

Demi-pension Room, breakfast and one main meal.

Density chart A reservation chart where rooms are shown in types only, e.g. singles, doubles. Common in larger hotels.

Departure list A list prepared daily showing rooms due to be vacated.

Deposit A prepayment by a guest to reserve accommodation.

Diary see Reservation diary

Disbursement An amount paid out by the hotel on a guest's behalf and charged onto his bill.

Doorman Employee who is at the front of the hotel to assist with luggage and taxis.

Double A room with one large bed for two people.

Double occupancy A room occupied by two people

Duty manager Member of the management team who is responsible for guest contact during his working hours.

Early departure A guest who checks out before his scheduled departure date.

English breakfast A full breakfast of hot beverage, bread, preserves, cereal and a cooked dish.

En pension see Full board

Eurocheque Could be described as a cross between a cheque and a travellers cheque. Written in local currency but drawn from the client's own account, like a cheque and backed with a Eurocheque card (limit usually £100 but varies from one country to another).

European plan Room only.

Fax A way of transmitting information in its original form through a British Telecom line—rather like two photocopiers linked by telephone.

Float Sum of money issued to staff to provide change.

Full board Bed, breakfast and two main meals. In some hotels, early morning tea may also be included.

Full rate A guest who is paying the full tariff for his accommodation.

Group inclusive tour (GIT) A package tour.

Guaranteed booking A booking for which payment is guaranteed whether or not the guest arrives.

Guest list see House list

Half board see Demi-pension

Head porter Senior porter, who supervises other porters and doormen.

High season Peak season, when prices are highest.

Hotel booking agent An agent who specialises in hotel bookings.

Housekeeper's report A report prepared twice daily showing the occupancy of each room.

House list A list showing the room number of every guest in the hotel.

In-house credit card A system of ledger accounts within an organisation or company which enables a client to charge an item to an account which is forwarded to them at a later date. Encourages customer spending and loyalty.

Key card A card or booklet given to a guest on arrival to show the room number and room rate.

Lead time The length of time between the booking date and the arrival date.

Linkman see Doorman

Low season Off-peak period of the year.

Luggage pass A release slip issued by the cashier to show that a guest has paid.

Luggage porter A member of the uniformed staff who takes luggage from the entrance hall to guests' rooms.

Maid's report see Housekeeper's report

Mail shot A circular sales letter usually used to inform clients of new developments or improved facilities.

Market segment Term used to describe the major sources of business to the hotel—i.e. business clients or tourists.

Modified american plan see Demi-pension

NCR (*a*) National cash register.

NCR (*b*) No carbon required; a form of self-carbonating paper.

Net rate A rate offered to wholesale travel agents which is net of commission.

Night audit Department working through the night, that carries out posting of charges and control duties.

No show Guest who does not arrive to take up a reservation.

Occupancy level The number of rooms that are let in a given period.

Off A room that is out of service for maintenance.

Overbooking The practice of accepting more reservations than there are rooms available.

Page A member of the uniformed staff who acts as a messenger for guests and callers.

Peak period see High season

Pick up A term used in machine accounting to denote the adding on of the previous balance on a guest's bill.

Posting Entering charges onto guests' accounts.

Prepayment Where a guest's bill is paid in advance of his stay.

Pre-registration Registration details of each guest on a tour are provided before they arrive at the hotel.

Prestel Two-way computerised information service for use with TV and telephone—thousands of pages of 'on screen' information sent via ordinary telephone lines. Used in travel agents/airlines etc.

Private automatic branch exchange (PABX) This system allows guests to dial their own telephone calls from the room without the assistance of the operator.

Rack rate see Full rate.

Rack slip A small piece of paper with details of the guest placed into the room rack at the front desk.

Reception office The department handling the checking in of guests, and room status.

Register A book kept at the reception desk where guests enter their name on arrival.

Registration card A card given to each guest on arrival to complete with details of name and address.

Release time Some reservations are held for guests, provided that they arrive before a certain time frequently 6.00 pm. If they do not arrive, then the room can be sold to another guest.

Reservation chart see Advance booking chart

Reservation diary A diary with details of all future bookings.

Reservation office A department that deals with all guest bookings.

Room board A board in the reception office showing the status of each guest room.

Room list see House list

Rooms division All the departments that are concerned with the accommodation of the hotel.

Safe deposit A facility offered to guests for the storage of valuable property.

Sales ledger Accounts of guests who have used the hotel and who have credit facilities.

Shift leader Member of front office staff in charge of shifts of employers.

Shoulder period A mid-price period between high and low season.

6 pm release The most common release time for reservations.

Sleeper A guest who stays overnight.

Split shift A shift where employers work two periods in a day with a rest break in the afternoon.

Stay on A guest who extends his stay beyond the original departure date.

Stop-go chart A chart in the reservation office showing at a glance whether space is available.

Stop list A list of stolen and invalid credit cards issued by the card company.

Studio A room that can be converted from a sitting room to a bedroom.

Suite An arrangement of rooms together, normally at least a sitting room, bedroom and bathroom.

Tab see Tabular ledger

Tabular ledger Handwritten summary of guests' accounts.

Tariff List of charges of the hotel.

Telex A system of transmitting written messages by telephone line.

Tour A group of people travelling together and staying in the same hotel.

Tour list Rooming list of tour members.

'Transient' hotel A hotel in which the guests are staying *en route* to another destination. The most common form of 'transient' hotel is the motor hotel. Hotels at ports and airports are often used by travellers waiting for travel connections and may also be classed under this heading.

Travel agent Agent handling a range of services, including travel reservations, hotel bookings, and theatre tickets.

Travellers cheque A cheque sold to travellers for use abroad that requires two signatures by the payee, one made in the presence of an issuing agent and one made when the cheque is cashed.

Twin Room with two single beds.

VAT Value added tax.

VDU Visual display unit.

VIP Very important person.

Voucher A form issued by travel agents to cover the cost of specified accommodation and meals.

VPO Visitors paid out. *See Disbursement*

Walk-out Guest who leaves the hotel without paying his bill.

Whitney rack Patented equipment that can show room status or advance reservations.

X key A key in the accounting machine that allows a trial balance to be read.

Z key A key in the accounting machine that allows the machine to be cleared when the balance has been proved.

INDEX

INDEX